CW00496042

OFF-R
IN THE
HEJAZ

Patrick Pierard and Patrick Legros

Published with the
support and encouragement of

Published by Motivate Publishing

Dubai: PO Box 2331, Dubai, UAE
Tel: (+971) 4 282 4060. Fax: (+971) 4 282 4436
e-mail: books@motivate.co.ae
www.booksarabia.com

Abu Dhabi: PO Box 43072, Abu Dhabi, UAE
Tel: (+971) 2 627 1666

London: Stewart's Court
220 Stewart's Road, London SW8 4UD
Tel: (+44) 20 7627 2481. Fax: (+44) 20 7720 3158
e-mail: motivate-uk@motivate-uk.demon.co.uk

Directors:
Obaid Humaid Al Tayer
Ian Fairservice

© 1997 Patrick Pierard, Patrick Legros and
Motivate Publishing

First published 1997
Reprinted 2001

ISBN: 1 86063 027 8

British Library Cataloguing-in-Publication
Data. A catalogue record for this book is
available from the British Library.

Printed by Rashid Printing Press,
Ajman, UAE

CONTENTS

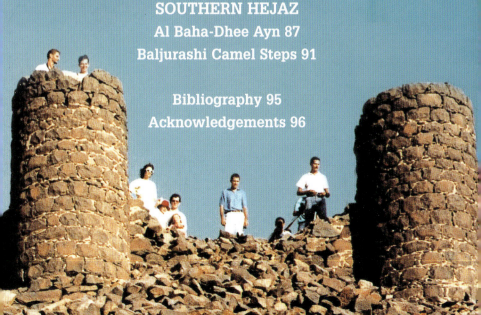

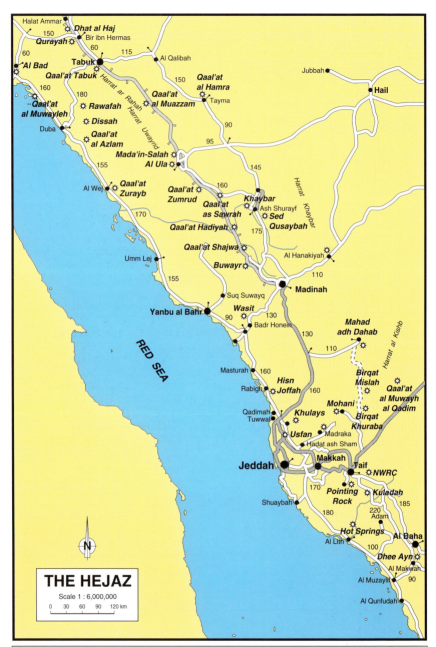

Halat Ammar
150 ☼ *Dhat al Haj*
Qurayah ☼ ● Bir ibn Hermas
60   60
60   115   ● Al Qalibah
☼ *Al Bad*   **Tabuk** ●   Jubbah ●
☼   *Qaal'at Tabuk*   150   *Qaal'at*
160   Harrat ar Rahah   *al Hamra*   ● **Hail**
☼ *Qaal'at* 180   *Qaal'at* ☼   Tayma
al Muwayleh ☼ *Rawafah* *al Muazzam*
Duba ●   ☼ *Dissah*   90
           Qaal'at   95
           al Azlam ☼
      Mada'in-Salah ☼
155   *Al Ula* ☼   145
Al Wej ● ☼ *Qaal'at*   Harrat
      ☼ *Zurayb* *Qaal'at* ☼   160   Khaybar
          Zumrud *Qaal'at*   *Khaybar*
170   *as Sawrah* ☼ ● Ash Shurayf
              Qaal'at Hadiyah ☼   ☼ *Sed*   *Qusaybah*
                                175
          Qaal'at Shajwa ☼   ● Al Hanakiyah ☼
Umm Lej ●   *Buwayr* ☼
155   110
              ● Suq Suwayq   **Madinah** ●
      Wasit
Yanbu al Bahr ● 90   ☼ 130
              ● Badr Honein
                        130   *Mahad*
RED SEA   *adh Dahab*
                        110   ☼
              Masturah ● 160
                    Hisn   *Birqat*
              Rabigh ● ☼ *Joffah* 160 *Mislah*   ☼ *Qaal'at*
                        Mohani ☼   *al Muwayh*
              Qadimah ● *Khulays* ☼   *Birqat* *al Qadim*
              Tuwwal   ☼ *Usfan* ● Madraka *Khuraba*
                    ● Hadat ash Sham
              Jeddah ●   **Makkah** ●
                        Taif ●
                        ☼ *NWRC*
                170
                    Pointing ☼ *Kuladah*
              Shuaybah ● *Rock*   185
                180   220
                        Adam ●
                    Hot Springs ☼
                    Al Lith ● ● **Al Baha**
                            100
                        Dhee Ayn ☼
                        ● Al Makkah
              Al Muzaylif ●   90
              Al Qunfudah ●

THE HEJAZ

Scale 1 : 6,000,000

0   30   60   90   120 km

FOREWORD

"See CAPRI... and die"! So they say in Europe. Here, in the Western Region of Saudi Arabia, you should say "See the Jebel Abiod and survive"!

This perfect ash cone of a white volcano, isolated by the black crust of Harrat Khaybar, is something I dream to see and later to guide visitors to. Unfortunately, the 105-km-long track approaching it, is presently such a nightmare that the geologists go there by helicopter. In this book, we do not offer you this first class 'Mount Fujiyama of Saudi Arabia' because our purpose is not to prepare you for an ordeal with a unique landscape feature as an aim. Many other beautiful landscapes or man-made historical structures of interest are now more and more easily reached by nature enthusiasts and drivers devoted to history and who are looking for a better understanding of the country. We trained ourselves with the basic 'Bushwalkers and Land Trekkers Bulletin' in hand and, step by step since 1988, we discovered that many marvels of Hejaz are not reserved for the happy few driving a four-wheel drive (4 WD) vehicle. For the last six years we managed to guide many families with 2 WDs to conspicuous peaks, along colourful wadis. On the way, a rock carving, an ancient dam, and caravanserai have been the trekkers' rewards. With this guide we care for the newcomer. We offer him road sheets as clear as the ones used by car rally drivers.

Take care with the mileage noted, as it may have a plus/minus of five per cent margin in accuracy because different cars have a different 'gauge' in this field and the tyre inflation also influences the tyre circumference. On a distance of more than 100 km you can gauge the ratio of your meter compared to the one of the road sheet. Then you can adjust the distance of your next landmark according to your car meter.

Every route presented in this guide has been carefully checked and re-checked by several teams. With the passage of time though, some elements such as roads or the landmarks we have used to give directions may change. We will be happy to hear from readers of such cases, so that future editions of this guide can be updated. Some parts of the Hejaz Railway were last checked a few years ago and this has been indicated next to the route.

Because this guide will be read and used by many, please leave only footprints and take only photographs where we guide you.

KEY FOR MAPS

	Freeway		Petrol station
	Main road		Traffic light
	Dirt Track		Car park
	Hejaz Railway		Recommended camping site
	Track on foot		Hejaz Railway station
↑ 5.3 ↑	Distances in kilometres		Watchtower
	2 WD circuit		Water tower
	4 WD circuit		Mosque
	Wadi		Haj caravanserai
	Major escarpment		Dam
	Lava area		Sightseeing spot
	Sabkah area		Quarry
	Hills		Palmgrove

MADRAKA VALLEY

Starting point: Jeddah north, airport royal terminal on Madinah freeway
Finishing point: Palm grove of Wadi Guran
Distance/Time: 300 km/one day trip
Category: Two-wheel drive
Highlights: A deep penetration inside the western fringe of the lava field to reach a green palm grove and walk downstream.

Within 160 km, east of Jeddah, you travel through the low hills in the middle of a geologist's paradise. Wildlife is part of the sightseeing. We observed parrots, weaver birds, a duck, a fox, baboons, a hyena and a wolf that had been killed by the shepherds and left hanging in the trees. Going eastward there are many areas of interest which can provide you with several day trips.

The farm area

North of Jeddah International Airport, the skyline is black, but the base of the long west-easterly range is reddish. The explanation of our expert in geology is that you observe the end of a lava flow when it is no longer a huge coat covering all the countryside, but it is reduced to a tongue winding along the existing wadi from that period. Now the relief is inverted. The former sedimentary hills have been washed away into the Red Sea pit and the former wadi, protected by a layer of lava, has become a conspicuous long ridge. On both edges of the lava tongue, earth is reappearing but baked and reddish due to the $1,500°C$ temperature of the lava when it was still liquid.

In between the road and the lava tongue lies a prosperous farm and you are about to see many from Usfan to Madraka. This first one, Rafia farm, is the private property of a grandson of King Abdulaziz and a son of King Khaled. It hosts an impressive array of lovely animals and birds, different species of gazelles and oryxes, Asian camels with two humps... Visits by families are possible by authorisation of the manager, provided that the Prince's family life is not disturbed. For the other farms on the way to Madraka, knock at the gate, ask for the manager, enquire about the vegetable or cattle food produced, but you must have an Arabic-speaking translator. In a farm with a circular irrigation system we were even guided by chance by the landlord from Makkah.

The Hadat ash Sham palm grove

Compared to the Al Ula palm grove, this one is not as huge and impressive as the most famous along the trade routes of Saudi Arabia, but, 100 km from Jeddah by road, you have a good sample of agricultural life where a wadi is wide enough to accept several square plots of land. Here grow alfa alfa, sorghum as a cattle fodder, tomatoes, green beans with reduced exposure to sun, thanks to lines of palm trees. In the middle of Wadi Sham, a rocky hill is protruding with a village at its base. On 10 January, 1992, this hill became an island for two days when it rained heavily. Somebody that day marked the compound wall in red at the highest water level.

Wadi Guran, during the January '92 flash flood.

Stand with your back to the wall to appreciate that everything below the level of your eyes was under water. You then realise how impressive the flash flood was on that day: all crops, wells and gardeners' huts were under the water's surface. At a well we suggest you take some time to speak with the gardeners to learn about their crops and their cattle, the variation of the water supply, the last flash flood they experienced and so on. At the other end of the palm grove, on climbing the harrat you experience a quasi-aerial view over the wadi and you can view through your binoculars the most colourful patches of cultivation below you.

Madraka

Unfortunately, this little town is not attractive because the palm grove seems to be drying up due to the rash pumping in the gravel bed downstream. The interesting parts of Madraka are few and, opposite the telecommunication tower, a very good graded dirt track crosses the harrat to join Birqat al Aqiq, 90 km further. Of course, this is for 4 WD only. The sight of the black lava plateau with some 'pimples' (old eroded ash cones) at half way gives a feeling of infinite dullness. The surprise is to discover Bedouin camps in the middle of nowhere. They make their living out of goats and sheep, provided they succeed in keeping wolves, hyenas and foxes away. It is a symphony in black.

Wadi Guran

Ten km further, beyond Madraka, the road runs along another palm grove without a village thereafter. On the left, a graded dirt track goes down into the wadi to cross it before the palm grove, where half of the year's rainwater runs on naked limestone. Provided the stream is not too high, this is a good ford for the Bedouins camping with their flocks on the huge harrat extending north of the wadi.

The palm grove is a nice place for a picnic and the start of a two-hour walk down the stream. The month of May is recommended because this is the month with the highest rainfall, when water flows from the escarpment. Within 50 m of the western edge of the palm grove, a flat rock

The Wadi Guran gorge.

8

displays an interesting rock carving, the 'shrieking baboon'. A photograph from the National Wildlife Research Centre (NWRC) in Taif confirms the capability of the baboon to have a mouth so wide open. Downstream the water running in the gorge of Wadi Guran appears very clear, because it has first been filtered in the gravel bed of the wadi before being compelled to reappear in the gorge where the wadi bed is of hard rock only, polished by the former flash floods. Where the flash floods have created a whirlpool, the rock is drilled and shaped like a pot. The children who have previously enjoyed the waterfalls along this wadi request this field trip every year.

How to get there – refer to Jeddah East map, page 10.

0   Departure from Royal terminal, Jeddah airport on Madinah road. Go north.
15 Take the first 'Usfan' exit, turning on to the ring road east.
17 Take the second 'Usfan' exit.
21 Rafia farm (private) on left-hand side.
22 Police checkpoint on right-hand side.
25 Horse racecourse on right-hand side.
41 'Two nipples' on right-hand side. Easy climbing and viewpoint.
44 Usfan Turkish fort on left-hand side.
46 Take the 'Shamya' exit, to be on the old Madinah-Makkah road heading south.
78 At the T-road crossing, turn left (east) towards Madraka.
82 'Al Fenaid' Farm with circular irrigation on left-hand side.
91 Long bridge. **Hadat ash Sham** palm grove starts at this bridge. On the left, 100 m after the bridge there is a platform big enough to park 60 cars.
97 Research farm on right-hand side after 2 km of graded dirt track, which breeds Arabian horses, cows and deer under sheds.
106 On right-hand side, nearly on top of the slope, look at an interesting cross section of a grey lava flow covering a reddish sedimentary layer.
139 **Madraka** village. Decaying palm grove. On right-hand side a graded dirt track goes south-east to **Birqat al Aqiq** across a 90-km-wide lava field. The track starts at the mosque with a square minaret, opposite a communication tower on left-hand side. The first 200 m are paved up to this minaret.
147 The asphalt road crosses a pass to jump into the next north-eastern valley.
149 The palm grove of **Wadi Guran** appears on your left. Before the palm grove, a platform on the south bank is big enough to park 20 cars. Two tracks lead to it, one before the safety rail in the middle of the curve, the other at the other end of the safety rail.

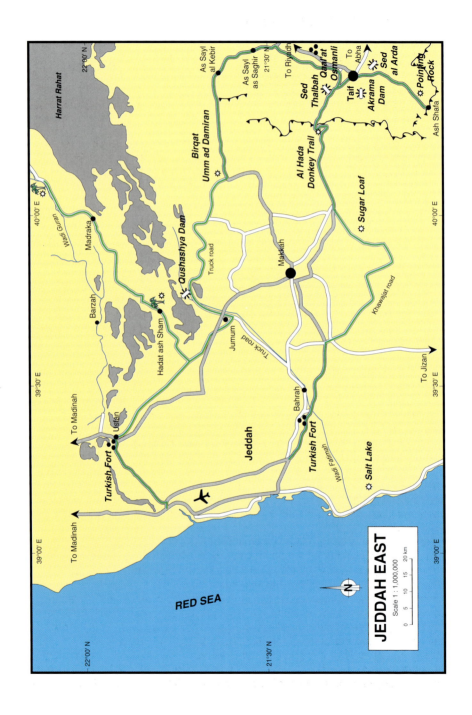

JEDDAH EAST

Scale 1 : 1,000,000

0   5   10   15   20 km

RED SEA

Harrat Rahat

To Madinah

To Madinah

Madraka

Barzah

Ustán

Turkish Fort

Hadat ash Sham

Qushashya Dam

Jumum

Truck road

Truck road

Jeddah

Bahrah

Turkish Fort

Wadi Fatimah

Salt Lake

Birqat
Umm ad Damiran

As Sayl
al Kebir

As Sayl
as Saghir

To Riyadh

Al Hada
Donkey Trail

Makkah

Khawajat road

Sugar Loaf

To Jizan

Sed
Thalbah

Qal'at
Osmanli

To
Abha

Sed
al Arda

Pointing
Rock

Taif

Akrama
Dam

Ash Shafa

Wadi Guran

22°00' N

21°30' N

22°00' N

21°30' N

40°00' E

39°30' E

39°00' E

39°00' E

39°30' E

40°00' E

N

10

TURKISH FORTS AROUND JEDDAH

Starting point: Jeddah north, police checkpoint on Madinah freeway
Finishing point: Qaal'at Usfan
Distance/Time: 280 km/one day trip
Category: Two-wheel drive
Highlights: a circular trip comprising four forts, made from the same black lava stone.

Among the Haj qaal'ats (pilgrimage forts) on the Egyptian route or north-western coastal camel trail from Yanbu al Bahr to Makkah is a chain of four interesting forts: Hisn Joffah, Qaal'at Khulays, Qaal'at Usfan and Qaal'at Dukhan. These massive structures have a number of architectural elements and other features in common:

- They are built with the same black lava stone.
- They have only one wall with a main gate; the other walls have two or three round buttresses looking like towers filled up inside. The top of the buttresses may have had a watchman position giving a lateral view and safe shooting capability against potential assailants climbing the walls with ladders – but only a complete buttress could tell us that for certain.
- Each of these forts was built on a high point, giving a good view of the surrounding areas; consequently there are no wells in the inner courtyard.
- They are located approximately 50 km apart, or a one-day camel ride for pilgrims travelling to the Holy City of Makkah.

Historical Background

The age of these forts is still undetermined until the Department of Antiquities completes its survey of this route, but we can guess that the four forts are at least 200 years old. Travellers' accounts tell us that the Swiss explorer, Jean-Louis Burckhardt (1786-1817) made a stop at Hisn Joffah in January 1815 on his way from Makkah to Madinah. He also visited Khulays and Usfan. In these faraway tiny garrisons life all year round was impossible for unpopular Turkish soldiers. Burckhardt mentions that at Khulays in 1815 the assignment was subcontracted to third country nationals (Moroccans) who were friendly with the local villagers. Some of them started a family life there before retirement from the Ottoman army. At Khulays the 'Egyptian' pilgrimage route is joined by a 'Syrian' route from Damascus and from time to time there was competition and rough brushing between the different communities. The detailed description by Charles Doughty (1874) gives an idea of the devoted, noisy crowd of pilgrims arriving at a qaal'at, buying goods from local traders. Doughty travelled part of the route with the pilgrims, and had first-hand experience in travelling with them: the setting up of camp each night, the folding of tents early in the morning at the first shot of the Ottoman military escort, the repeated attacks by the local irregulars killing or robbing the stragglers, as well as the purification rites performed before approaching Makkah. At the arrival of the caravan, the forts were for the Turkish escort cavalry only, providing them with rest and food. The wealthy pilgrims went

At Khulays, the location of the pilgrims' tents, where basalt rocks have been removed, is clearly visible in the foreground.

to their tents which had been pitched earlier by their servants as close as possible to the fort.

Hisn Joffah

Even though its northern wall has been destroyed, Hisn Joffah is better preserved than its sister forts at Khulays and Usfan and we recommend you visit it first. Located 9 km south-east of Rabigh, the drive is an easy 1½-hour trip from Jeddah along the salty Tihama coastal plain. Once you reach the area around the fort, however, the terrain changes and becomes sandy with gravel. In some places creamy sand dunes form high drifts. Wadi al Halq runs southward here and the view from the wadi bank is beautiful; the valley spreads outward below, from where, in the distance, the misty form of Jebel Farasan can be seen.

Hisn Joffah stands solitary among the sand dunes, an obvious beacon to the weary pilgrim. It is a rugged, massive fort, its remaining three walls jutting upward on the wadi bank. Finger-like sand streaks reach up the sides of the fort, contrasting sharply with the black masonry of the lava stone walls. The northern wall, where the gate used to be, has collapsed. The fort is about 40 m x 40 m. An interesting feature of Hisn Joffah is the 11 high arches supporting the watchman's gallery on the southern wall; from this vantage point, soldiers were well warned of impending assaults and the approach of travellers coming to stay for the night. The inner courtyard is open and could accommodate a military force of some 50 men with their horses or camels. Since there is no well, it is most likely drinking

12

water came from Bir al Jafa, 2 km south of the qaal'at, which is now Joffah Meegat, a religious site where pilgrims perform necessary rites before entering Makkah.

Qaal'at Khulays

As you approach Khulays, you can see the angular shape of Qaal'at Khulays on top of a round hill coated with black lava overlooking the northern bank of Wadi Khulays. To capture the spirit of the pilgrims of the old days, you must set out and climb that lava hill like them, anxious as they were to spot the site of the stage camp long before they reached it, and to enjoy a night's rest in peace and safety near the castle walls. The square boulders covering the hill, which resemble a heap of giant toffees well shaken in their box before being dropped across your path, is a result of the lava-cooling process when the surface contracted into a fragmented crust. Mind your ankles when climbing up this black mess – and also watch your speed when coming down. We recommend starting the visit from the quarry where you park your car at the south-west tip of the hill, shortly after the hamlet of Al Aziziyah. Upon reaching the top of the toffees' you encounter a Turkish outpost, meant for observing the blind area around the hill on behalf of the main fort at the other end of the table land. Like relieved soldiers after their night watch in the outpost, you then reach the fortress by following the flat ridge up to a saddle before the last spur supporting the Ottoman qaal'at.

Near Qaal'at Khulays some pilgrims' tent locations are still visible – nice platforms of soft ground cleared of lava rocks.

Water was not available in the qaal'at but more than abundant in nearby Wadi Khulays. Archaeologists have discovered the remains of a dam south of the fort. Donkeys carried as much water to the fort as was necessary. The problem of the Khulays area was, in fact, the excess of water rather than the shortage; in 1975 a flash flood destroyed 90 per cent of the farms along the wadi path and washed away 25 cm thick of top soil. A dam was envisaged for Wadi Marwani in the gorge upstream, but the sedimentary banks with lava crust are a poor base to fix a dam and the project was cancelled. Availability of water is appealing for the huge thirsty town of Jeddah. To supplement pumping already installed in Wadis Fatimah and Ash Sham, Al Ayn al Aziziyah Company was created in 1965 and 65 per cent of the water extracted from Wadi Marwani-Khulays is now forwarded to Jeddah. The water requirements are now driving pumping as deep as 40 m instead of 2 to 8 m as in the old days. This means that water is more and more salty, a major concern for the local villagers of a formerly rich agricultural area.

Qaal'at Usfan

Fifty km south of Khulays at the 'Jeddah' exit of the Makkah freeway, you cannot miss Qaal'at Usfan, in the middle of a freeway interchange on a mole hill. Its shape is similar to that of the other forts. The size, however, is reduced to 20 x 25 m. Inside the fort you can explore a vaulted cellar with a crumbling entrance. Do not expect ammunition in this safe place, but we have sometimes encountered hundreds of bats in that room, much to the pleasure of the children. Bring a flash light for the visit.

Qaal'at Dukhan

For some time we were looking for this missing link half-way between Usfan and Makkah. We were searching too close to Jumum. By chance, in 1996 we were discussing about history with an extremely knowledgeable Saudi farmer who explained to us his present work on the restoration of an old qanat (underground canal) system 15 km north of Jumum. When we mentioned our interest for old forts, he observed that he had one on his farm area, looking like the Usfan one. Straight away from Birqat Tandub we went to look at it: the ruins showed us a true copy of Usfan on a small hillock dominated in the north by an extension of the Harrat Rahat lava plateau. Permanent availability of fresh water at the base of the harrat was the reason for a caravan stopover protected by a fort slightly outside the direct line from Usfan to Makkah. The square Birqat Tandub and the circular Birqat al Fayja (diameter: 100 m) are on the way from the Taif truck road to Qaal'at Dukhan and demonstrate the importance of this last staging area before Makkah.

How to get there - refer to Jeddah North map, page 15.
We recommend a circuit of the three forts north of Jeddah according to the following data sheet. **Qaal'at Dukhan** is so similar to Qaal'at Usfan that we leave you the pleasure to look for it at the base of Harrat Rahat, 16 km north of Jumum and 5 km off the Taif truck road by a good graded dirt track, via Birqat Tandub.

- 0 Departure from the petrol station on Madinah freeway just before the north-Jeddah police checkpoint.
- 55 Take exit No. 32 to Tuwwal.
- 57 T-road crossing. Turn right (north) to Yanbu.
- 75 Interchange with bridge. Keep straight.
- 78 Sabar police checkpoint. Keep straight.
- 98 Cement factory. Keep straight.
- 102 Power line crossing. Keep straight.
- 106 Road crossing. Turn right (east) to **Joffah Meegat.**
- 112 Turn left (north) into a very good graded dirt track going to a gypsum quarry.
- 118 Turn right into a Bedouin dirt track leading to a visible dark ruin.
- 119 **Hisn Joffah** (Qaal'at Olaya in some books).
- 0 Reset your milometer. Take the graded dirt track and asphalt road back towards Makkah and south.
- 7 Turn right (west) into the Jeddah-Joffah Meegat asphalt road.
- 13 Turn left (south) into the Rabigh-Jeddah road.
- 43 Take the 'Makhah' road at the bridge interchange junction.
- 58 Pass under the bridge of the Jeddah-Madinah freeway, going towards Khulays.
- 70 Cross a power line on top of a lava field.
- 74 Road crossing in a hamlet. Turn left (east) towards Khulays. The square fort starts to be noticeable on a round spur.

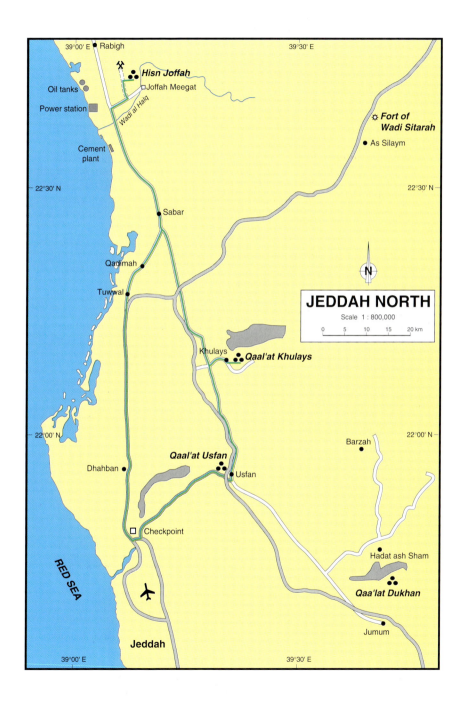

39°00' E • Rabigh

⚒

● Hisn Joffah

□ Joffah Meegat

Oil tanks ●

Power station ■

Wadi al Halq

☼ Fort of
Wadi Sitarah

● As Silaym

Cement
plant ▮

22°30' N

22°30' N

● Sabar

Qadimah ●

Tuwwal ●

JEDDAH NORTH

Scale 1 : 800,000

0   5   10   15   20 km

N

Khulays
●● Qaal'at Khulays

22°00' N

Barzah ●

22°00' N

Qaal'at Usfan
●●●
● Usfan

Dhahban ●

□ Checkpoint

Hadat ash Sham ●

RED
SEA

✈

●● Qaa'lat Dukhan

Jeddah

● Jumum

39°00' E

39°30' E

39°30' E

80 At the end of asphalt road at Al Aziziyah village, turn left towards the second water tower in the village, drive along a graded dirt track used by the water tank trucks.

83 Turn left into a private dirt track going to a roof protecting a disused power generator. Park nearby under the trees, south-east of **Qaal'at Khulays**. Start walking towards a noticeable small ruin at the beginning of the slope south of the fort. 100 m before the ruin, have a look at a short dam (15 m) creating a temporary birqat (reservoir) for the fort garrison in the rainy season. Like the soldiers of years past, climb the slope towards the fort, but the donkey track is washed away. When you go 10-15 km further east on the graded dirt track, you enter the Wadi Marwani gorge denting the harrat. There are then many camping areas on the banks of the wadi. Select the very high ground to pitch your tent if you do not want to be washed away by an unpredictable night's rain. Two families were rescued by a Civil Defence helicopter in January 1992 on a Friday afternoon and, one week later, they recovered their vehicles and gear in good condition thanks to the safe location of their camp and the kindness of the local shepherds.

0 **Qaal'at Khulays** car park. Reset your milometer. Go back west by the same graded dirt track.

3 You are on asphalt road. Go on west towards the Makkah-Jeddah freeway.

8 Road crossing with the old Madinah-Makkah road. Petrol pump on right-hand side. Keep straight.

11 Pass under the freeway bridge and turn left (south) towards Makkah by the freeway.

46 Take 'Jeddah' exit and park your car on the right-hand side along the fence of a camel farm. **Qaal'at Usfan** is on the left. Be very cautious when you cross the freeway at the curve. Climb the mole hill from the northern side up to the fort courtyard. The sightseeing finishes here and you now go back to Jeddah.

Haj route and valley of Usfan

Collapsed rubble

Vaulted room

QAAL'AT USFAN

0   10   20 m

Courtesy of ATLAL

73 Turn right (west) into the Jeddah east ring road.

75 At the interchange on the Madinah-Jeddah freeway, take the 'Jeddah' turning to enter the city.

SUGAR LOAF

Starting point: Jeddah, south-east exit on Makkah freeway
Finishing point: Sugar Loaf
Distance/Time: 160 km/one day trip
Category: Two-wheel drive
Highlights: the Sugar Loaf pinnacle rock.

On the way from Jeddah to Taif, a 70-km-long road bypasses Makkah, the Holy City forbidden to non-Muslims. When the escarpment wall is in sight, a pinnacle protrudes from the low hills. Long before it was climbed by the Natural History Society Trekking Club, it was given the name of 'Sugar Loaf'; this long 5-kg solid piece of sugar is still very much in favour amongst the Sahara nomads. The trick in climbing it is to use the 'back door'. A reconnaissance showed that, if the roadside face of the rock is vertical, the other side has a convenient slope. Over a height of 3 m at the beginning of the climb, you need to use your hands/fingers to go through a crack. From then on it is an easy 50-m-high ascent, winding up to the top. From there you will enjoy an all-round view with some Egyptian vultures flying over you. The birds' nest is in a hole on the vertical face and they seem to be puzzled by the fanatics who crave for a bird's-eye view of the wadis.

The Sugar Loaf with an exceptionally clear Sarawat range in the background.

17

The recommended access to the rock is a 7-km-long walk in the flat sands, after leaving your car on the road side. For families with babies who want to join you for the picnic, an 11-km Bedouin track to the base of the rock is accessible by 2 WD. The area is still very low in altitude (300 m), so summer weather can be unpleasant there. The recommended period to enjoy the 'Sugar Loaf' is from the end of November to the middle of February. Outside that period it is no longer rambling, but special force training!

The thumb-like Sugar Loaf.

How to get there – refer also to Jeddah East map, page 10.
    0 'Longines' petrol station at the exit of Jeddah on Makkah freeway.
  38 Take the 'Taif-Shumaysi' exit obligatory for non-Muslims.
  80 Before Mira poultry farm, turn right on to a dirt track accessible to 2 WD leading to the base of **'Sugar Loaf'**. Or better...
81.5 After Mira poultry farm (+ 1.5 km), park your car on the left side of the road and start a 7-km-long walk, leaving the main ridge on your left.

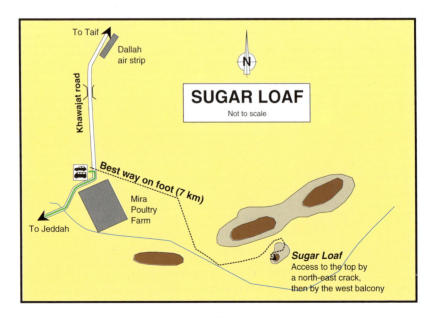

WADI ASH SHAFA

Starting point: Jeddah, south-east exit on Makkah freeway **Finishing point:** Le Caillou Qui Bique (The Pointing Rock) **Distance/Time:** 380 km/one day trip **Category:** Two-wheel drive **Highlights:** roadside marketstalls; Jebel Daka; watchtowers seen from the pointing rock.

During any season when Jeddah residents want to exercise in the mountains, Wadi Ash Shafa at 2,000 m high offers a pleasant climate. When it is cold in winter, it is easy to protect yourself with a light sports jacket. Taking a poncho in the backpack is not unwise because three of our 40 trekking parties there, have finished under a downpour with waterproofs on. The freeway brings you to the edge of the escarpment. The end of the road is the Shafa ring road around a charming hamlet, with four watchtowers and an old cemetery dating back from before Wahabism. In the summer the Shafa loop is so popular and crowded that the police order the traffic one way on the two existing lanes along the loop and many drivers feel like competitors in a chariot race in a Roman circus. For a rest from the crowded road, stop at some of the roadside stalls, bustling with early morning trade. It is where the local farmers sell their fresh vegetables and fruits, from colourful carrots to prickly pears. From time to time 'flower men' from Asir appear to sell their honey. Jebel Daka at 2,585 m high overlooks Wadi Ash Shafa and its microwave tower can be reached by a curling road. It is of little interest because it has no impressive view of the escarpment. Our favourite goal in the area is a prominent hill crowned by an odd-looking boulder in the shape of a pointing hand. "The French have already been, seen, conquered and named it 'Le Caillou Qui Bique' (The Pointing Rock) after a similar Belgian landmark at Roisin close to the Belgian-French border. In deference to fellow Europeans and a stronger currency, I won't even attempt to rename it," wrote Mark Watson in 1992, a keen trekker from the Jeddah British Council.

'Le Caillou Qui Bique' (CQB) or The Pointing Rock

The trekking circuit lasts three hours including a one-hour picnic below the summit. You leave your vehicle in a car park attached to a recreation area. From the car park on the top of a ridge you have a complete view of the circuit and are in a position to observe the main features of the landscape – historical, geological, or even zoological.

You start your trekking cross-country, aiming for a perfect watchtower to the south-west. That tower is the best among the eight you will be able to locate around you from 'Le Caillou Qui Bique'. These towers have nothing to do with the Turkish control of the Hejaz from 1600 to 1919, the year the Madinah Turkish garrison surrendered in the aftermath of the First World War. In the not-so-distant past the mountain villages were constantly fighting each other. Producing the crops was so hard and time-consuming that the natural trend was to get them – already processed and

The 'Caillou Qui Bique', the Saudi counterpart of a famous Belgian pointing rock.

free of cost – with a little bravery, by plundering from the closest store. The natural reaction of the farmer was to fortify the store and to watch the usual path on which the intruders would arrive, from the top of the store. So today you can see the product of the 'hard work' of those dedicated farmers – complete with their white quartz ornamentation. Many of the towers are at least 200 years old and are worth a picture.

Before reaching the first tower, you have to pass by a small farm with women working around. Be nice, show yourself on the last ridge and by the time you have organised a competition for the first one to find a scorpion under the stones, the farm children will have noticed the new intruders and informed their mothers so they can take cover. They are entitled to their privacy and this does not mean they do not have a sense of hospitality. Sometimes the farmer invites your party for a cup of tea and he is not daunted by 20 guests.

From that watchtower, look for a goat trail winding its way towards the fields on the right-hand side of your target, the CQB at approximately 2,150 m above sea level. You can negotiate the CQB hill by its southern slope and the final ascent from the field to the top is a little less than 100 m high. The assault on the hill is a scramble over and around huge, smooth and densely-packed granite boulders. After a picnic under the beckoning summit, a mere 20 m above your head, the volunteers can creep up a narrow 8-m-long 'chimney' leading to the base of the CQB. It would be so nice to have it decorating a Jeddah roundabout! On one of our visits, a climbing demonstration was given by a Navy commando officer using his fingers and the tip of his toes on the 6-m-high surface of the final rock, but this was not repeated on

An euphorbia in the middle of granite rocks.

21

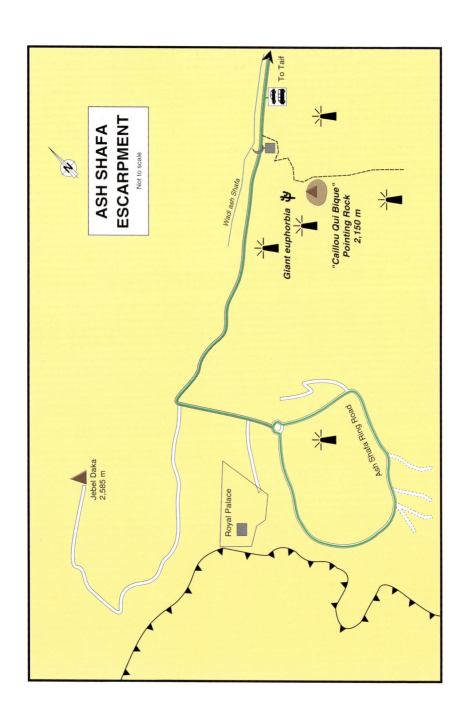

ASH SHAFA ESCARPMENT

Not to scale

To Taif

Wadi ash Shafa

Giant euphorbia

"Caillou Qui Bique"
Pointing Rock
2,150 m

Ash Shafa Ring Road

Royal Palace

Jebel Daka
2,585 m

subsequent visits. For safety we regularly equip the 'chimney' with a mountain guide rope to give confidence to those who experience vertigo on the way down rather than on the way up. From the base of the 'chimney' we usually get down on the eastern slope commonly used by the goats and the young villagers who climb the CQB barefoot on that side. At the base, in the wadi flowing east, do not miss a hollow granite boulder providing shade for a group of up to 20 people. The goats pass under it, and so can you without having to bend. Going on east in the field you can follow a good dirt road bringing you back to your car. Look out for the colourful ladies working in the fields. Their head-dress is black and flat on the top without a veil on the face. The gown is embroidered like a Moroccan kaftan and stops at the knees. Below the gown appear long bright leggings, red, blue or green.

To finish the circuit you still have to stop at the last farm of the 'bowl' on the left side of the dirt road. Close to the abandoned white building there is a giant euphorbia which sprouts in the shape of a thick rigid bouquet. Several other smaller euphorbia transport you towards other landscapes like those appearing in 'Tintin in Mexico'. Over the six-year period we have visited this site, we have encountered two living snakes, many colourful birds and lizards. A black snake as thick as a thumb disappeared slowly under a boulder in the first rocky farm area. Seen only by the tail at a 3-m distance, it was not identified by the leader of the group, but this sighting is common to all rocky areas, even in Europe. The rule is simple: walk slowly, do not give the feeling to the snake that you are aggressive, leave that to the mongoose!

How to get there – refer also to Jeddah East map, page 10.

0	'Longines' petrol station at the exit of Jeddah on Makkah freeway.
38	Take the 'Taif-Shumaysi' exit obligatory for non-Muslims.
105	Take the 'Obligatory for non-Muslims and Taif' exit. You are back on the freeway after the Makkah bypass.
125	Police checkpoint at the base of the escarpment road.
150	Police checkpoint at the top of the escarpment road. Go through Al Hada pass and go down towards Taif.
165	Turn right at the 'Shafa' exit on the Taif western ring road.
179	Turn right at the 'Shafa' exit to enter the **Wadi ash Shafa** freeway which takes you again to the great escarpment.
192	On your left a holiday village made of a new mosque and white huts appears, covering the slope up to the ridge. Turn left just before the mosque and park your car on the ridge after 100 m uphill.

AL HADA DONKEY TRAIL

Starting point: Jeddah, south-east exit on Makkah freeway
Finishing point: Al Hada donkey trail
Distance/Time: 270 km/one day trip
Category: Two-wheel drive
Highlights: Roman-style paved pathway.

To reach Taif from Jeddah, the shortest way is to drive along the escarpment road climbing the 2,000 to 2,500-m-high Sarawat range. When you are two-thirds of the way along the 25-km-long uphill road, 3 km after a microwave tower on the left side of the road, zigzags appear on the opposite side of the valley. You discover the best section of an ancient trade route referred to by the Makkah residents as the 'donkey trail'.

Historical background
Many foreign travellers made the Jeddah-Taif trip in the old days, but few left a good account of their hardship on this trail. In 1815, Jean-Louis Burckhardt was invited to Taif to meet Mohammed Ali, viceroy of Egypt, who was based there to lead his conquest of Yemen. "We reached some

Snaking down along the Al Hada donkey trail.

A male baboon deters a potential competitor.

huts named Kahwet Kora. This being the shortest road from Makkah to Tayf, caravans are continually passing. The camel loads are deposited at this place, and then forwarded to the summit of the mountain on mules and asses, of which two hundred are kept here. The more northern road to Tayf is passable for camels all the way; but it is by one day longer than this. We found the road very steep. Steps had been cut in several places and the ascent rendered less steep, by conducting it, in many windings to the top: half a dozen of spacious resting places had also been formed on the side of the mountain, where the caravans take breath ...". So is described the donkey trail in 'Travels in Arabia' by Burckhardt.

A pleasant walk
After several tests on different sections of the donkey trail, we selected the middle one, where hikers can enjoy a pleasant walk along Roman-style stone-paved pathways. Leave the car in a huge parking area at 1,050 m high, overlooked by a fine stone building, which once accommodated a road

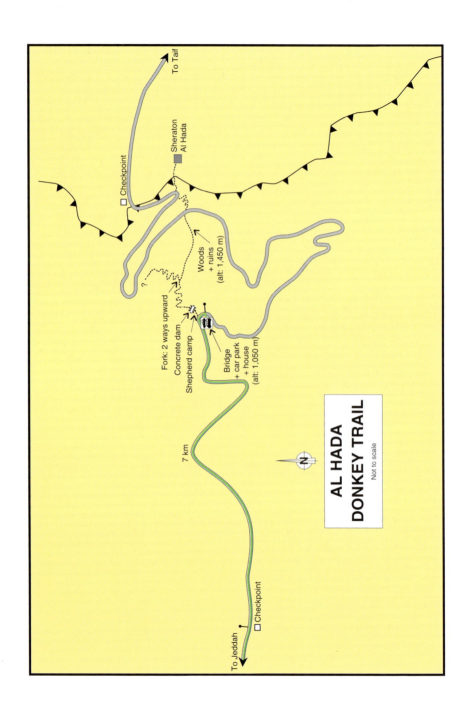

To Taif

Checkpoint

Sheraton
Al Hada

Woods
+ ruins
(alt: 1,450 m)

?

Fork: 2 ways upward

Concrete dam

Shepherd camp

Bridge
+ car park
+ house
(alt: 1,050 m)

7 km

AL HADA
DONKEY TRAIL

Not to scale

N

Checkpoint

To Jeddah

26

maintenance team. From this platform formed by a curve of the new road and an opposite curve of the old road, you cross the heavy traffic road safely by going upstream under a wide bridge and you stay in the wadi for 2 km in order not to disturb the shepherd family who are permanently camping astride this first leg of the donkey trail. When you meet a concrete dyke across the wadi, you ascend the rock at the base of it on the left-hand side along the junction of the wall with the slope. Half of the year, the rainwater stored in the gravel bed behind the dyke creates a nice stream which cascades for 500 m to the pleasure of the goats and their masters. Above the dyke three huge ficus sycomorus wait for you and offer their generous shade. After a rest, go south for only 50 m, to find the smooth flat stones of the donkey trail. You are now 100 m higher than the car park and you are recommended to go another 300 m higher to enjoy your picnic under one of the many acacias. When the trail disappears on the south bank, you can see its retaining wall reappearing on the north bank, so you have to cross the wadi bed. Later, at a fork after a natural balcony, you can choose your way. The right branch of the fork has a rather quick end in the wadi bed under a road bridge. We recommend that you take the left branch along the narrow zigzags so conspicuous from the road, on the opposite side of the valley. The many windings lead you to a saddle and a spur from which the view of the Tihama plain is spectacular. The trail goes further to another saddle, 50 m beneath the escarpment road then it disappears totally. Most probably, the modern roadworks have wiped out the old track.

After lunch, on the way down to the car park, you are more relaxed to watch the male baboons fighting for the control of their females, the blue agamas sunning themselves on top of the rocks, and different types of cacti, either long fingered with tiny yellow flowers or with strong square section branches and purple velvet flowers as big as a fist (caralluma russeliana).

For the complete 400-m climb, untrained but fit people will need two hours. We recommend the period from October to April. A quiet walk down takes 1½ hours.

How to get there – refer also to Jeddah East map, page 10.

0   'Longines' petrol station at the exit of Jeddah on Makkah freeway.
38   Take the 'Taif-Shumaysi' exit obligatory for non-Muslims.
105   Take the 'Obligatory for non-Muslims and Taif' exit. You are back on the freeway after the Makkah bypass.
125   Police checkpoint at the base of the escarpment road. Go on for 7 km.
132   In a curve to the right, below a road maintenance team building made of well-trimmed limestones, a platform between the present road and the opposite curve of the old road offers a safe car park for 200 cars. From the car park to the **donkey trail** upstream we recommend that you cross the fast traffic road by walking under the main bridge.

NATIONAL WILDLIFE RESEARCH CENTRE

Starting point: Jeddah, south-east exit on Makkah freeway
Finishing point: NWRC/Taif
Distance/Time: 430 km/one day trip
Category: Two-wheel drive
Highlights: the houbara bustard; oryx; ostrich; educational workshops and films showing the NWRC's wildlife programmes.

Historical background

The Saudi Minister of Foreign Affairs, HRH Prince Saud Al Faisal, a self-proclaimed reformed hunter, realised that unless action was taken the houbara bustard may cease to be a breeding species in the Kingdom. He discussed a breeding programme with French businessman Jacques Renaud and in 1985 the first houbara chick was hatched in Kintzheim, France.

The ibex, a past king of the Sarawat range.

Encouraged by this success, HRH asked Renaud to set up a houbara bustard captive breeding facility in an area south of Taif where houbaras are known to have once bred. The National Wildlife Research Centre (NWRC) came into formal existence in 1986, initially with the purpose of breeding in captivity and releasing houbaras back into the wild in Saudi Arabia.

Concurrent efforts towards habitat protection and recovery were also necessary in order to create areas in which houbara could be released. In addition, it was understood that the houbara bustard, though a flagship species under which other wildlife could receive protection, was by no means the only example of endangered native wildlife in Saudi Arabia. Uncontrolled hunting and the loss of natural vegetation through overgrazing by domestic livestock had resulted in the

The houbara bustard, the favourite prey of the falcon.

decline or extinction of a number of Arabian species. Most notable of these were the Arabian oryx and the Arabian examples of ostrich, cheetah and wild ass, all extinct in the wild, and the Arabian leopard, a species persecuted to the brink of extinction. The status of other, lower-profile animals such as the wolf, caracal, hyena, and gazelle, and birds such as the Arabian bustard and lappetfaced vulture was also uncertain; not to mention a host of plants, invertebrates, reptiles and even fish. Clearly what was urgently needed in Saudi Arabia was a comprehensive national programme of habitat protection and restoration.

    In late 1986 the National Commission for Wildlife Conservation and Development (NCWCD) was created to oversee wider conservation programmes in the Kingdom. The NWRC was designated as one of the Commission's research centres, the others being the King Khaled Wildlife Research Centre (KKWRC) at Thumamah, and more recently the Wildlife Sanctuary for the Gulf Region at Jubail. KKWRC occupies the farm of the late King Khaled and provided the first Arabian oryx for the breeding programme at the NWRC. Currently the KKWRC is responsible for the conservation and restoration of the gazelle and ibex populations. The Jubail Gulf Sanctuary grew from an oiled sea bird rehabilitation centre, set up to cope with the disastrous consequences of the Gulf War oil spills.

This ibex procured from the San Diego Zoo is the best friend of the visiting children.

30

Today the work of the NCWCD, based in the old Ministry of Foreign Affairs building in Riyadh, follows an ambitious plan to create and manage a system of protected areas in Saudi Arabia. To date, there are 10 reserves protecting over 50,000 sq. km, with the ultimate goal of protecting as much as eight per cent of Saudi Arabia. There are a number of species-specific reintroduction programmes for the Arabian oryx, ostrich, rheem and idmi gazelle, and of course the houbara bustard. The NWRC now has responsibility for the captive breeding and reintroduction of the oryx, ostrich and houbara with plans to breed the onager, the nearest relative to a wild ass that inhabited the Arabian Peninsula. Along with the breeding and release programmes, the NWRC also supports research and monitoring projects on endangered carnivores, endemic and native birds, bats, reptiles and baboons and even vegetation and insects. As the Commission's representative in the south-west of the Kingdom, the NWRC also receives sick, injured or orphaned animals for treatment by the veterinary staff, and intermittently takes in caracals, wolves, hyenas, mongooses, porcupines and other rarely seen animals.

The NWRC sits within 10 sq. km of protected natural vegetation. This core reserve is surrounded by an electric fence to prevent entry by any unwanted visitors such as red foxes, which may create havoc in the houbara breeding unit. Within the reserve are the Centre's offices, laboratories, staff housing, workshops, breeding cages for the houbara, and fenced enclosures for the oryx. To prevent the spread of disease from domestic livestock to the oryx, the NWRC is surrounded by a non-grazing buffer zone, extending the total protected area to 80 sq. km. After nine years of protection from sheep, goats and camels, the vegetation within the NWRC's fence has recovered remarkably. The contrast between the interior and the overgrazed exterior is striking.

The key to the restoration of wildlife in Saudi Arabia lies to a large extent on successfully raising the public's awareness of conservation issues. This requires an understanding of the benefits of protected areas to maintain the natural balance and to preserve the diversity of nature for the enjoyment of future generations. To this end the NWRC has a vigorous programme of public awareness, and runs its own video unit to create short films about the Centre's work. A selection of these films may be viewed by visitors to the Centre.

How to visit the Centre

Visits and tours of the NWRC are by appointment only. The Centre is not a public facility with regular scheduled tours, therefore staff must be taken off their normal duties to lead groups. This is usually not a problem and visitors are welcome, but at least two weeks' notice should be given so that a suitable time can be arranged. Visiting groups should be between five and 15, though smaller or larger groups may be accommodated.

People wishing to arrange a visit to the NWRC should contact the NWRC director at the following numbers:

Tel: 02-745 51 88 (working hours) Fax: 02-745 51 76 (all hours).

NWRC staff will try to accommodate visits during both weekends and normal working hours (8 a.m. to 6 p.m. Saturday to Wednesday and 8 a.m. to 12:30 p.m. on Thursday).

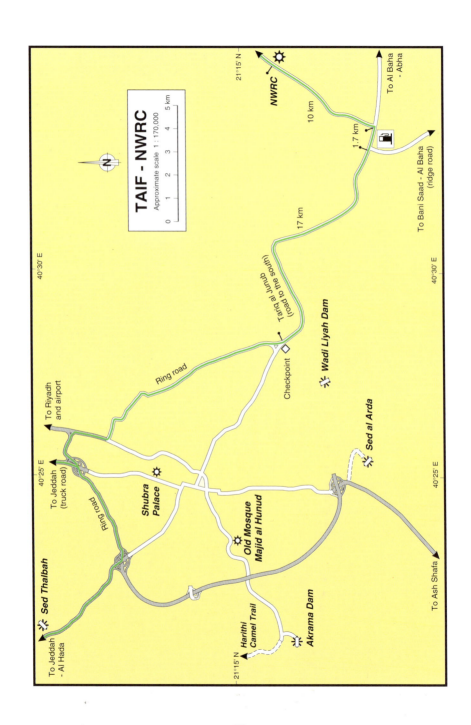

TAIF - NWRC

Approximate scale 1 : 170,000

0   1   2   3   4   5 km

N

21°15' N

NWRC

To Al Baha - Abha

10 km

1.7 km

To Bani Saad - Al Baha (ridge road)

40°30' E

17 km

Tariq al Jumub (road to the south)

Wadi Liyah Dam

Checkpoint

Ring road

To Riyadh and airport

Sed al Arda

40°30' E

40°25' E

To Jeddah (truck road)

Ring road

Shubra Palace

Old Mosque Majid al Hunud

To Ash Shafa

40°25' E

Sed Thalbah

Ring road

To Jeddah - Al Hada

21°15' N

Harithi Camel Trail

Akrama Dam

The following animals may be viewed at any time: houbara bustards, Arabian oryx, Nubian ibex, onagers, gazelles.

Other animals such as hares, Arabian hedgehogs, snakes, bats, birds and small reptiles roam freely within the protected area, but are generally not seen before sunset.

How to get there – refer also to Jeddah East map, page 10.
- 0 'Longines' petrol station at the exit of Jeddah on Makkah freeway.
- 38 Take the 'Taif-Shumaysi' exit obligatory for non-Muslims.
- 105 Take the 'Obligatory for non-Muslims and Taif' exit. You are back on the freeway after the Makkah bypass.
- 125 Police checkpoint at the base of the escarpment road.
- 150 Police checkpoint at the top of the escarpment road.
  The Al Hada ring road on the right (+50 m) leads to Sheraton Al Hada, convenient for those who want to have a night's rest in the mountain before starting the drive along the picturesque ridge road to the south (This 3-km-long bypass to the Sheraton is not included in the total mileage).
- 166 Take the 'Airport-Riyadh-Sayl Al Kebir' exit when you meet the Taif ring road.
- 173 Access on matar (airport) road at the Ordnance Corps Maintenance School. Turn right towards Taif centre for 800 m up to a traffic light giving access to the north-east section of the ring road up to Tariq al Junub (road to the south).
- 182 Police checkpoint east of Taif. Take direction 'Abha'.
- 202 Dangerous crossing: leave direction 'Bani Saad' to your right and take direction 'Abha'.
- 203 T-crossing: turn left (east) to 'Sudayrah-NWRC' (please note: the colourful signpost is sometimes missing).
- 213 **NWRC** is to your right after a long fence doubled by an earth bank protecting wild species from car headlights at night.

A viper, under Taif NWRC control.

33

QAAL'AT AL MUWAYH AL QADIM

Starting point: Jeddah, south-east exit on Makkah freeway
Finishing point: Qaal'at al Muwayh al Qadim
Distance/Time: 800 km/a weekend trip
Category: Four-wheel drive
Highlights: Qaal'at Osmanli; rock carvings; Qaal'at al Muwayh al Qadim.

Historical background

The Turks first came as pilgrims to Makkah and Taif, as early as the 13th century. By the 18th century they had established their administrative control over the Hejaz, when Taif became the summer capital of the Vali (Governor) of the Vilayet (province) of Hejaz. In 1802 their garrison was wiped out by the Nejd warriors spreading Wahabism. Between 1811-1813 Muhammad Ali, Ottoman viceroy of Egypt and a former Albanian soldier of fortune, organised the recapture of Taif. From that base, the viceroy and his son Ibrahim Pasha led decisive operations in 1818 to destroy Diraiyah, the capital of Nejd in the east and again in 1834 in order to gain control of Asir and Yemen in the south.

We have fairly good descriptions of the Taif garrison by Jean-Louis Burckhardt, the Swiss explorer invited there in 1814 by Muhammad Ali, later by Maurice Tamisier, a French employee of the Egyptian-Turkish medical service in 1834 and by Charles Didier, a fellow-traveller of Richard Burton in 1854. The huge Bab al Ri citadel, a three-storey and four-tower castle, known by a 1899 photograph, had been purposely destroyed around 1934 but, outside Taif, there are still conspicuous remains of the Ottoman military architecture:

- an Osmanli Qaal'at in the Arafat rest area, 23 km north-east of the Intercontinental hotel, on the southern side of the Taif-Riyadh freeway. This may be a picnic stop under the trees south-west of the fort.
- a black lava cubic caravanserai on the northern edge of the Hafir village on the way from Radwan to the Wabah crater.
- the Al Muwayh al Qadim fortified caravanserai, 42 km north-west of the new Al Muwayh village built on the Taif-Riyadh freeway.

Qaal'at Al Muwayh al Qadim, King Abdulaziz hunting lodge

Along 90 per cent of this 400-km journey from Jeddah, you will be travelling on a high speed freeway before finishing the last 10 per cent by stepping back into the old traditional cameleer civilisation. Al Muwayh al Qadim is a black-lava-stone caravanserai on Darb al Hejaz (the caravan route from Riyadh to Taif), where it skirts the southern edge of Harrat al Kishb. To reach this qaal'at you have to cross some 42 km of soft hills if you take the track starting at the eastern exit of new Al Muwayh. Alternatively, you can take a bearing of 335 degrees (N-NW) at the very entrance of the village's main street, bypassing the Taif-Riyadh freeway to the north, but be ready to spend half of your driving in the fluffy soil of the Al Ashariyah salt lake. During a rainy period, stay away from those western tracks as they are awfully muddy, and take the gentle hilly track farther east. On the way, you will meet Oteibi tribesmen and their predominantly black camels. If you have any doubt about the right track, since there are many, Oteibis will show you the right direction. You will know you are very close when you see a black square lookout tower on the top of a gentle grey sedimentary hill. The 100-m-wide Qaal'at Al Muwayh is concealed just behind the tip of that low ridge. You have the feeling of being at the edge of the 'Desert of Tartars' (Italian novel by Dino Buzzati), where a poor young lieutenant became old and sick just by waiting for the appearance of the invisible enemy. You discover an impressive, sturdy building with six square watchtowers, some with machicolation. The west and east gates have a perfect round arch wide enough for access to any modern vehicle, with a watchman's room over them.

Both Doughty (1878) and Huber (1884) made a stopover at these wells, but neither of them mentions a fort. So most probably this structure with gates wider than the usual caravanserai is less than 100 years old.

If the local rogue Bedouin watchman has no objection (our ratio is 50 per cent bad luck), you can visit and discover the four phases of the fort development in the last 90 years:

- An original small square fort 20 x 20 m, with four round towers, one at each corner, as a core.
- A bigger rectangular fort, some 70 m long, with five square towers, one being the western gate. This extension creates an important courtyard around the small fort, although 30 m of the eastern wall have been erased to build a water or petrol underground supply station.

Al Muwayh al Qadim, a caravanserai converted into a hunting lodge.

- A northern extension adds an independent courtyard and a double row building looking like an officer's quarter, with its own tower-gate and several windows opening to the outside of the compound. Up to this stage of construction the architecture looks very much Turkish and uses black lava stones.
- A southern extension to the small fort is the well-known plastered diwan. The inside consisted of a long row of official seats facing a wide meeting room with a terraced roof supported by many square section pillars. This accommodation was built some 60 years ago by the late King Abdulaziz ibn Saud to welcome the local Amirs (tribal chieftains), his new subjects, when he was escaping the Riyadh protocol. He even landed here with his Dakota twin-engine aircraft.

The qaal'at is so close to the dry salt lake that you can imagine its western wall reached by the high waters of the exceptional rains as may happen once in every ten years in the area. At such times the caravanserai is isolated from the opposite 10-m-high edge of the lava flow by a 600-m-wide temporary lake.

The hunting activity of King Abdulaziz is left to your imagination because gazelles, oryx, houbara bustards and ostriches have been overkilled by the advent of new hunting methods using 4 WD vehicles. In between the qaal'at and the lookout tower on the ridge, the slope is covered by an abandoned mud-brick village which accommodated the royal suite of cooks, drivers and servants of bygone days. An airstrip including a terminal was able to receive the royal Dakota for a quick visit to the hunting ground. The rusty bodies of the trucks used to increase the hunting range of the Shahin (falcon) are still there for everyone to see. The water table is so close to the surface that in the gullies of the salt lake indenting the harrat, there are several wells attracting not only the travelling cameleer but also partridges and doves, themselves an easy prey for the foxes.

This trip is possible in a day, including five hours of driving from Jeddah, a one-hour picnic at Al Muwayh al Qadim and five hours to drive back to Jeddah. But we strongly recommend, for your enjoyment, that you camp in the area somewhere on an elevated location. Rain is unpredictable!

How to get there – refer also to the Hejaz map, page 4.

    0 'Longines' petrol station at the exit of Jeddah on Makkah freeway.

  38 Take the 'Taif-Shumaysi' exit obligatory for non-Muslims.

105 Take the 'Obligatory for non-Muslims and Taif' exit. You are back on the freeway after the Makkah bypass.

125 Police checkpoint at the base of the escarpment road.

150 Police checkpoint at the top of the escarpment road.

162 View of the light brown wall of the Thalbah dam 1.5 km north of the road, (easy to see when you are driving from Taif to Al Hada pass).

166 Take the 'Airport-Riyadh-Sayl Al Kebir' exit when you meet the Taif ring road.

173 Access on matar (airport) road at the Ordnance Corps Maintenance School. Turn left towards Riyadh.

180 Intercontinental Hotel on your left.

196 Police checkpoint.
203 **Qaal'at Osmanli**, a Turkish fort in the Arafat rest area on your right. Refreshment stop recommended under the trees south-west of the fort. Rock carvings showing animals along 400 m of the ridge north of the road, opposite the qaal'at, behind a fence. Carvings visible with binoculars. Recommended rest stop on your way back.
303 Radwan (here a dirt track heads north leading to Wabah crater).
332 Mahazad as Said signpost (a national wildlife reserve south of the freeway).
360 Take the 'New Al Muwayh' exit. Before entering the village, take an immediate bearing 335 degrees (N-NW) bypassing an animal souk to the west.
380 The brownish flat bottom of Sabkah al Ashariyah appears on the left. On the right, the light grey ridge starts with four separate hillocks. That gentle low ridge has its northern tip at Al Muwayh al Qadim.
398 When the dark black edge of the lava flow is in sight, look for a conspicuous black square watchtower on the eastern ridge on the right.
402 At the lookout tower, **Qaal'at al Muwayh al Qadim** is 500 m below you.

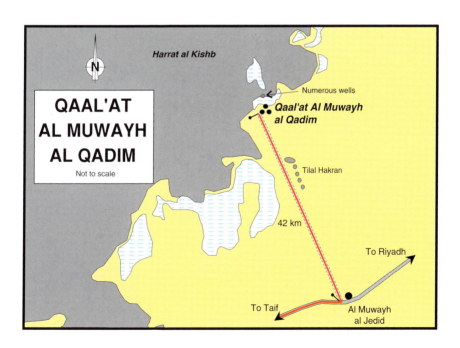

37

MADA'IN-SALAH

Starting point: Jeddah north, police checkpoint on Madinah freeway
Finishing point: Mada'in-Salah archaeological site
Distance/Time: 1,600 km/ 2/3 days
Category: Two-wheel drive, or air and bus
Highlights: Jebel Ethlib; Harrat Rahat lava field; Nabatean tombs; Islamic fort; the Hejaz Railway.

Who would dare to contest the title of sightseeing spot No. 1 of Saudi Arabia to Mada'in-Salah?
There are so many reasons to be attracted to this area:
- The natural beauty of the landscape is made by the contrast between the green trees surrounding the numerous wells of the valley and the round reddish sandstone pinnacles of Jebel Ethlib.
- Under the name of Al Hijr, Mada'in-Salah is a very ancient stopover on a trade route of a highly successful commercial empire, which spread from Alexandria and Aleppo in the north to Yathrib (Madinah) in the south.
- A religious mark has been carved here deep in the sandstone by the Nabatean nomads, who aimed to achieve a stable afterlife in impressive tombs.
- A second religious mark is left here in the form of an Islamic fort, providing welcome rest and protection to the Haj pilgrims, half-way

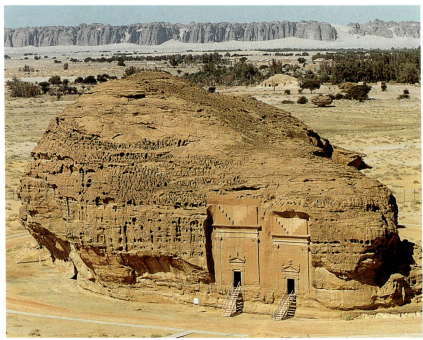

An island of eternal peace in a sea of sand.

Qsar Farid, the photographers' favourite.

between Damascus and Makkah, before the machine age.
- Your visit also includes samples of a technical achievement, the Hejaz Railway linking Damascus to Madinah as early as August 1908. A global view of this subject is given in a special section (see page 55).

The Frankincense road

Under that name a camel trail joined the Indian Ocean in the south to the Mediterranean Sea in the north. Aromatic resin scratched from the Hadramaut shrubs, spices from India, lapis lazuli from Afghanistan and gold from the Kingdom of Saba were the precious loads carried by the camels. Pharaonic Egypt was craving for frankincense: up to 700 kg for one festival, one temple, one day to please the gods and their priests. Mada'in-Salah with its many wells was a favourite rest place for the cameleers. Guiding the caravans from one well to the next, protecting the goods against other plunderers was a profitable business for the Bedouin who understood quickly that 25 per cent of the value of a durable flow was better than 100 per cent of the first caravan and nothing later. The Nabateans (500 BC to 100 AD), an Arab tribe, were not the first to practise the trade, but in history they appear as the first to have made a visible and lasting profit out of it. Here at Mada'in-Salah the proof of their success is not brilliant palaces but monumental tombs.

Incense route at Al Ula near Mada'in Salah.

The Nabatean religion

The Petra connection is obvious and well known. At Mada'in-Salah you are at the southern base of the same commercial empire, practising the same cult, worshipping gods represented in stone like Dushera and his female trinity, Allat, Al Ozza and Manat the goddesses. The eastern side of the archaeological site is dominated by Jebel Ethlib, a 2-km-long ridge made of successive round sandstone pinnacles. Its northern tip, Al Diwan (Arabic for the meeting room of the chief), is the main worshipping area of the site. There you find a wide open room hewn in the rock on the southern side of a narrow gorge leading to the religious complex. Before the room was

40

cleared of the sand which had amassed over the centuries, the French Dominican fathers Jaussen and Savignac from the Jerusalem Institute guessed that this was a funeral restaurant similar to the one at Petra, so the cave should have a triclinium, a three-sided stone bench along the wall base. Their estimates of 1907 proved to be correct in 1980. Following the south wall of the gorge, you discover many religious signs, betyls ('house' of god) or niches featuring a round top and two urns, with 1, 2 or 3 erected slabs inside (representing one, two or three goddesses, usually of different heights), basins to collect the blood of a sacrifice, petroglyphs over your head, rectangular meeting places formerly paved with marble or precious metal and eventually a stairway leading to the ridge. Your easy climb is rewarded with a wide view towards the west extending to the Islamic fort in the north and Qsar Sani tomb in the south.

The northern wall of the gorge is also interesting. Look for other betyls, an eight-cubic-metre rainwater tank carved in the rock supplied by a long channel also carved in the cliff, and an altar. From the top end of the sandy thalweg, the more daring can climb some northern pinnacles up to crude watch stations of the First World War period. The view extends far away over the northern plain.

The Nabatean tombs
The tombs made Mada'in-Salah attractive for a British traveller some 120 years ago. Charles Doughty came here in 1877, after he heard a lot about them in the Damascus coffee shops when discussing with the pilgrims coming back from Makkah via Mada'in-Salah. The Hajjis mentioned inscriptions appearing over the tomb doors. Compared to Petra, this is a

plus. Doughty received the authorisation from the Turks to join a Haj caravan and, as a Christian, promised not to go further than Mada'in-Salah. Doughty took two months to impress the Nabatean writings on wet blotting paper. The dried impressed paper sheets were sent to Ernest Renan in Paris, a Semitic language specialist and philosopher. The Nabatean writings are tomb property deeds. They refer to well-known Nabatean kings. They allow a clear dating of the tombs from 100 BC to 75 AD. This is the end of King Aretas IV's reign, 'the one caring for his people'.

The individual compartments inside the tomb.

41

We leave to you the pleasure to discover the ornamental beauty of the tombs, opposite stairways, eagles, griffins, snakes, human masks, rosettes, etc. At least three tombs appear to have suddenly been stopped at the level of the opposite stairways carving, the work always starting from the hill top. Obviously the profitable trade had dried up around 100 AD. The success of one attracts the greediness of others. The entrance of the Nabateans in history dates back to 312 BC, when Alexander the Great's successors made attempts to get hold of the Nabatean wealth in the north. Antigone of Macedonia and Ptolemy I of Egypt approached Petra, but they were either flatly beaten back or kept away by gifts in silver. The Greek greediness was followed by a Roman one, from Scaurus in 62 BC to Antonius and Cleopatra, his famous Greek-Egyptian partner, in 36 BC. Nabatean courage and diplomacy met with the same success against the Romans. In 24 BC, Aelius Gallius, Roman Governor of Egypt, led a force along the frankincense route down to Najran but his legion got lost on the way and starved. Alas, in 106 AD, the Nabatean resistance was overcome when Emperor Trajan's troops paraded in Petra. Most probably the Roman rule over Arabia Petrae was carried out by a commercial blockade, the effect of which became noticeable at Mada'in-Salah around 75 AD, but no Roman influence appears on the archaeological site proper.

Islam and Mada'in-Salah

Even though they had lost much of their splendour during the 7th century AD the Nabatean settlements in the Tabuk-Tayma-Al Ula-Haql polygon could not be ignored by the new monotheistic faith. In several surats, the Holy Qur'an records the process of conversion as difficult. The stone worshippers are called Thamuds, who in fact are the predecessors of the Nabateans in the area and left many rock carvings on the mountain slopes. The Thamuds were so reluctant that they killed the best sign of God's benevolence sent to them, a pregnant she-camel giving milk to all the community. So like Sodom in the Bible, Mada'in-Salah, the cities unconvinced by Salah, met their day of doom for refusing to hear the right way explained to them by Salah. An awful desert storm wiped them out, leaving behind only their tombs. This did not prevent the numerous wells of Al Hijr from becoming again a welcome resting place for the Syrian Haj pilgrims on their way from Damascus to Makkah, but this is another story deserving a complete trip (see page 71).

How to visit Mada'in-Salah

The site is fenced and under permanent police surveillance. No visit is possible without the following documents:

- A special nominative authorisation from the Department of Antiquities and Museums in Riyadh (PO Box 3734 Riyadh 11481 – Tel: 01-411 57 77 Ext. 233 - Fax: 01-411 20 51). This document is easily obtained by request, in the form of either a sponsor's letter or a fax, mentioning name, occupation, citizenship, Ikamah No. (resident identity card) and passport No. Application should be made one month in advance, but some visitors kindly get it by fax within a week. Make a few photocopies of your authorisation to be safe.

- A travel letter from your sponsor to go through the Madinah police checkpoints on the way.
- Ikamah or passport (for visitors with a temporary visa).
- Recommended for the road travellers:
  - Michelin map No. 954.
  - Zaki M.A. Farsi atlas: the Madinah bypass for non-Muslims is well explained.

A good visit requires a four-hour tour at the end of the afternoon to have a good view of the monuments facing west and a four-hour tour early the next morning for the monuments facing the sunrise.

A proposal for the weekend is:

Thursday
- Arrival at the site entrance for lunchtime.
- Lunch and camp setting as close to the gate as possible, but not in a wadi bed. Mind the rain in any season.
- Around 3 p.m. enter the site and visit:
  - Qsar Al Bint, the girl's house
  - Al Diwan
  - Al Madbah
  - Qsar Al Farid, the tomb selected for most of the Mada'in-Salah posters
  - Khasraf tombs.

Friday
- Get up early to climb the hill south-west of the site gate before sunrise.
- Observe the sunrise over Jebel Ethlib and the soft light then covering the whole site.
- Have your breakfast, then visit:
  - Qsar as Sani
  - Al Fahad tombs
  - Khurimat tombs
  - the main Nabatean well
  - the Islamic fort
  - the Hejaz Railway station and workshop.

When to travel to Mada'in-Salah

The best period in the year to visit the site and to camp is March-April and October-November. December, January and February can be very cold and it can snow on Jebel Ethlib, even if only once every 20 years. May to September is hot, but acceptable because you have plenty of shade all around the monuments and you are never far away from your air-conditioned vehicle.

How to travel to Mada'in-Salah

Transport and accommodation can be solved by several combinations during a two-day weekend, starting from Jeddah.

1) With a 2 WD car and hotel accommodation in Madinah:
   - Wednesday: leave Jeddah at 5.00 p.m.
   - Arrive at 9.30 p.m. at Madinah Sheraton.
   - Thursday: leave Madinah at 7.00 a.m.

At 9.00 a.m., take a break at Qusaybah dam south of Khaybar.
At 12.00 noon, arrive at the gate of Mada'in-Salah. Picnic in the
shade of Qsar Farid and make a quick visit up to 6.00 p.m.
Return to Madinah Sheraton, arrival around 11.00 p.m.
- Friday, late breakfast and departure around 10.00 a.m. towards
Buwayr railway station (see page 63) for a picnic. Back to Jeddah to be
home around 9.00 p.m.
Recommendation: to have two drivers for the same car to avoid
excessive driving stress along 1,800 km in 52 hours.
2) Air and bus with accommodation in the Madinah Sheraton for groups of
more than 15 people:
- Wednesday evening, take the last Jeddah-Madinah flight.
- Thursday, same programme as (1) above, but you enjoy the relaxation
of being driven in a comfortable bus with a great view on both sides
of the road.
- Friday, same picnic at Buwayr railway station (see page 63) and back
to Madinah airport for a flight to Jeddah late in the afternoon.
3) Air and bus with accommodation in the Tabuk Sahara hotel:
- Wednesday evening, take the last Jeddah-Tabuk flight.
- Thursday, same programme as (2) above, with the same assets.
- Friday, visit Tabuk in a rented car for four to five persons and take the
last Tabuk-Jeddah flight in the afternoon.
4) Air and bus and camping accommodation provided at Mada'in-Salah by
a reliable travel agency:
- Thursday morning, take the first Jeddah-Madinah flight. The bus is
waiting for you at Madinah airport. Lunch in a new Khaybar
restaurant. Arrive at Mada'in-Salah gate around 3.00 p.m. The camp
is prepared while you visit the monuments facing west. Barbecue at
the camp site.
- Friday morning, visit to the monuments facing east from 7.00 a.m. to
11.00 a.m. At 1.00 p.m., lunch in a new Khaybar restaurant. Visit
Buwayr railway station (see page 63). Back to Madinah airport for a
flight to Jeddah late in the afternoon.
This last formula with a good guide was very much appreciated
in 1995.

How to get there by road – refer also to the Hejaz map, page 4.

0   Petrol station and police checkpoint north of Jeddah on Madinah road.
70 Beginning of Harrat Rahat, the huge north-south lava field approximately
    100 km wide, filling a fault parallel to the Red Sea.
127 Exit No. 23 for Wadi Sitara. Stay on the freeway for a further 3 km.
    Hamlet without signpost with a petrol pump and a mosque, called
    Schleem/Sitara by the locals. After the pump, a narrow asphalt road goes
    east through the hamlet and winds down a thalweg.
    Wadi Sitara Turkish fort at the eastern edge of the lava plateau, north of
    your road (+ 1.5 km away from the freeway, not included in the mileage).
    In the main thalweg, go south 500 m further.
    Wadi Sitara caravanserai and birqat partly concealed by acacias in the
    wadi bottom (+ 2 km away from the freeway).

44

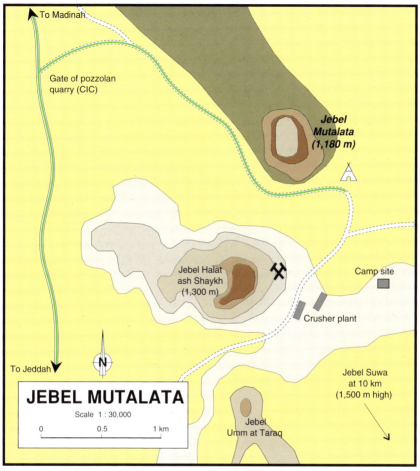

To Madinah

Gate of pozzolan
quarry (CIC)

Jebel
Mutalata
(1,180 m)

Jebel Halat
ash Shaykh
(1,300 m)

Camp site

Crusher plant

To Jeddah

JEBEL MUTALATA

Scale 1 : 30,000

0   0.5   1 km

Jebel Suwa
at 10 km
(1,500 m high)

Jebel
Umm at Taraq

213 After a bridge turn right at a gate with a 'CIC quarry' signpost. Take this
     graded uphill dirt track for a visit/camping at **Jebel Mutalata** (+ 3 km after
     the CIC gate. This optional stopover is not included in the Mada'in-Salah
     distance).
     The small volcano is immediately north of the graded dirt track. The
     higher one south is **Jebel Halat ash Shaykh** (1,300 m at the top, 120 m
     higher than Mutalata). Both are worth climbing as a volcanic experience.
     Go back to the freeway to proceed towards Madinah.

363 Police checkpoint south of Madinah. (see map, page 46) Take the west
     ring road at a traffic light 1.3 km after the checkpoint, direction 'Tabuk –
     obligatory for non-Muslims'.

366 Roundabout, turn right (north) into the ring road.

375 Road crossing (Yanbu road on your left, Holy City on your right), go
     straight towards Tabuk (and airport).
     Take the 'Madinah city centre' exit on your right if you go to the

45

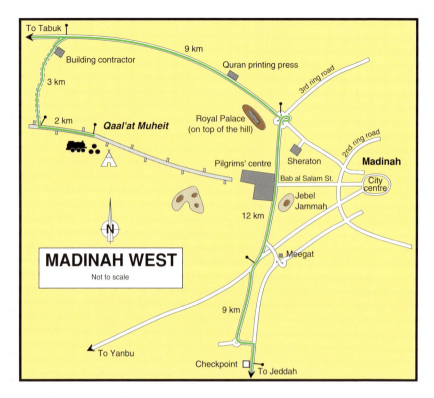

To Tabuk

9 km

Building contractor

Quran printing press

3rd ring road

3 km

2 km   *Qaal'at Muheit*

Royal Palace
(on top of the hill)

2nd ring road

Pilgrims' centre   Sheraton   **Madinah**

Bab al Salam St.   City centre

Jebel Jammah

12 km

MADINAH WEST
Not to scale

Meegat

N

9 km

To Yanbu

Checkpoint ☐   To Jeddah

Sheraton (the hotel is 1.5 km east of the interchange, on the right after the first traffic light). The Sheraton extra mileage is not included.

385 Take the 'Tabuk' exit after the bridge over ring road, turning right to go west.

394 Turn left into the short paved road if going to **Qaal'at Muheit** for camping.

406 Police checkpoint north of Madinah on Tabuk road.

410 Turn left into a paved road (+ 400 m) with a sign 'Hafirah' if you are going for a break at **Hafirah CFH** station at 4 km (mileage not included).

528 Turn right into a roughly asphalted track if you are going to **Qusaybah dam** (2 km west of the Tabuk road) for a break or camping (see page 85).

558 Al Wadi traffic lights and Turkish restaurant. Stay on freeway towards Tabuk.

586 Turn right (west) at the 'Al Ula' exit.

759 Turn right (north) at the 'Tabuk' exit, passing Al Ula by the east. New road in a scenic dry valley overlooked by nice sandstone pinnacles, made to reach the archaeological site by the shortest way.

783 Turn left (west) at the 'Al Ula' exit if you intend to base your camping at the **'Mammoth' stone arch** at 9 km from that exit.

794 Turn left (west) at the 'Mada'in-Salah Antiquities' exit.

801 Turn right (north) into a paved road towards 'Antiquities'.

802 Entrance of the **Mada'in-Salah protected archaeological site** and police station. We wish you a pleasant visit.

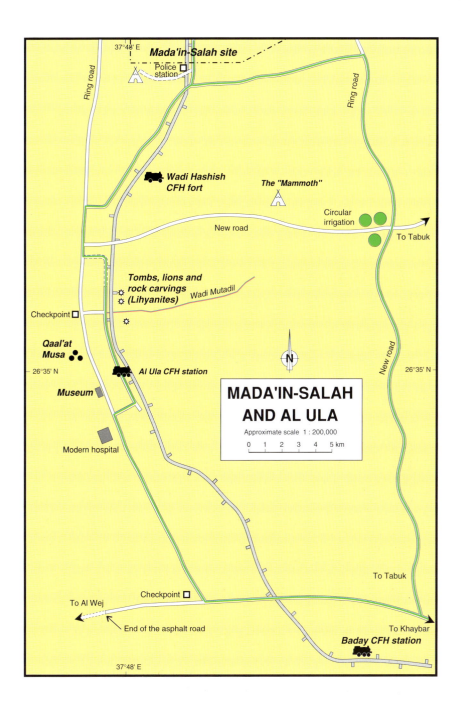

37°48' E

Mada'in-Salah site

Ring road

Police
station

Ring road

Wadi Hashish
CFH fort

The "Mammoth"

Circular
irrigation

New road

To Tabuk

Tombs, lions and
rock carvings
(Lihyanites)

Wadi Mutadil

Checkpoint

Qaal'at
Musa

26°35' N

Al Ula CFH station

New road

26°35' N

Museum

MADA'IN-SALAH
AND AL ULA

Approximate scale 1 : 200,000

0 1 2 3 4 5 km

Modern hospital

To Tabuk

To Al Wej

Checkpoint

End of the asphalt road

To Khaybar

Baday CFH station

37°48' E

47

AL ULA

Starting point: Mada'in-Salah, archaeological site
Finishing point: Al Ula
Distance/Time: 40 km/one day trip
Category: Two-wheel drive, or air and bus
Highlights: Al Ula's old abandoned city; sandstone pinnacles; oven tombs of the Lihyanites; museum; the Hejaz Railway.

The old abandoned city

Once you have adopted a conservative attitude, for example wearing trousers in the town instead of shorts, you can start the visit of the old abandoned city. It lies at the south-western edge of the loveliest palm grove we know. In the narrow valley overlooked by red sandstone cliffs and pinnacles, a medium-sized natural tower is crowned by an ancient wall with the name of Qaal'at Musa. The last part of the stairway leading to the top has disappeared, so there is no need to describe the old tomb of the holy man buried there because only helicopter pilots can view it. An easy climb halfway up the rock gives you an excellent view both north and south over the roofs of the old town and over the heads of the palm trees.

The Lihyanite tombs

In the red cliff on the north-east side of the valley, well above the palm tree tops, black square holes puncture the surface. These are the 'oven' tombs

The old abandoned Al Ula minus the minaret is certainly not very different from the Dedan city described in early writings.

48

of the Lihyanites, the predecessors of the Nabateans (1,000 to 500 BC). Just over the top of the row of tombs are two lion statues which are hewn into the rock as keepers of the dead Lihyanites. When the gate of the protecting fence is open, a new stairway (1993) leads you through the slope up to the base of the cliff where the 'lions' are. When you have the authorisation from the Department of Antiquities and when you find the doorkeeper with the proper key, you are able to climb that stairway to have a closer view of the 'lions' and a bird's-eye view of the huge Al Ula palm grove. The first condition is easy to meet, the second one is more difficult and you may be reduced to using binoculars. These tombs and several others are located at the entrance to a lateral wadi named Mutadil and the southern tip of that entrance is said to have plenty of petroglyphs, both Lihyanite and Thamud, but their access is restricted to authorised scholars. A museum in the town is said to explain the succession of cameleer civilisations in this fertile valley blessed by God with a permanent availability of water. During our weekend trips however we have never managed to find the museum doorkeeper.

The oven-like tombs.

The Hejaz Railway
Two stations are along the rail bed running on the eastern side of the palm grove. Al Ula, during the railway period, was a major Turkish army headquarters of the size of Madinah and Tabuk. It seems that several houses around 80 years old have benefited from the Syrian masons' skills during their off-duty hours, because several farm stone gates in the palm grove have the Syrian style of the railway forts. This is pure guesswork because the off-duty activities of the masons are not recorded in the

49

Two lions of stone watch over the tombs.

Turkish army archives, of course. The second station, Wadi Hashish, is at the north-eastern end of the palm grove. You have to look out for it behind a few palm trees, but you cannot visit it because it has tenants.

Camping in the area
As for the Mada'in-Salah visit, we recommend that you camp half-way between the two sites, at the 'Mammoth' stone arch. No need to be strictly close to it, because it is a popular place for the local youths who meet there to sing and play music late in the evening. But there are cosy spots nearby, with a sunrise or sunset view on this exceptional stone arch.

How to get there
Use the same mileage chart as Mada'in-Salah (see page 44). **Al Ula** is 20 km south of the Nabatean archaeological site.

NABATEAN SETTLEMENTS

Starting point: Tabuk Hejaz Railway Station
Finishing point: Rawafah temple, Dissah tomb, Al Bad tombs and Qurayah farms
Distance/Time: 410 km (Dissah) + 560 km (Al Bad)/one 2-day trip
Category: air and four-wheel drive
Highlights: sandstone hills with lava crust; water springs; oleander and lemon groves;archaeological sites; canyon with wadi; Bronze Age village; cross-country walls.

Historical background

The Petra and Mada'in-Salah rock tombs have made the Nabatean civilisation famous. Could it be that these two brilliant centres of civilisation, which lie 800 km apart, are separated by a no-man's-land? Nature is said to be averse to emptiness. So the Nabatean culture has also filled the gap between the north and south strongholds of this cameleers' commercial empire. Tabuk is the epicentre of several Nabatean settlements. For a long weekend trip you could fly to Tabuk on a Wednesday evening and rent a 4 WD at Tabuk airport. This allows a Jeddah resident to squeeze in a visit to four archaeological sites: the Rawafah temple, the lonely Dissah tomb, the Al Bad tombs and the Qurayah farms deserve a visit, if you intend to extend your knowledge on this long-lost but brilliant civilisation (see map, page 54).

Rawafah temple

Leaving Tabuk towards the west by the new Duba road (1990), at the end of a table land, at a distance of 105 km from Tabuk, a simple signpost in Arabic indicates the start of a Bedouin track going south to the Nabatean Temple of Rawafah. You drive for the next 21 km through a high grass area giving you the feeling that you are somewhere in the Far West, expecting to see more wild bulls than camels! You will pass by red cliffs with numerous rock carvings which are said to be 3,000 years old or more. As there are many tracks, you will probably want to confirm your directions every time you meet a Bedouin. They will answer readily and are eager to help.

The four ruined walls of the Rawafah temple are still 5 m above ground level. The lintel with Nabatean and Roman markings is no longer there to allow you to make your own dating of the 13 x 11 m building. It is said to be dedicated to Marcus Aurelius in the year 166 AD, after the Romans took control of the Nabateans. The trimming of the limestone is faultless. Its location in a wide saddle makes this monument conspicuous from the valleys on both sides now, as it was in the past. Its appearance from a distance gives a feeling of relaxation to the weary traveller. All around, the sandstone hills are covered by a decaying lava crust, resembling pieces of cake with a chocolate coating.

Dissah tomb

As the crow flies, Dissah village is only 15 km from the Rawafah temple, but the easiest way to reach the entrance of Wadi Qaraqir is to go back to the Duba road and to drive south for a further 9 km. Then you leave the asphalt road again to follow a busy 50-km-long graded dirt track.

Dissah is a Howeita village controlling the entrance to a red sandstone gorge where water springs are numerous at the base of towering pinnacles. Oleander, palm trees and lemon trees benefit from this constant water. A Nabatean cameleer had his roots here and his pride lay upon impressing his countrymen with a tomb as stylish as the one of the wealthy families at Mada'in-Salah. Two archaeological sites are fenced in the village. You will have to go around them to have a view of the lonely tomb. Friends have indicated several other places of interest in the area; old kilns, Aramean rock carvings etc. For a specialist Wadi Qaraqir deserves a month-long visit, guided by a Howeita friend.

Al Bad tombs and Qurayah farms

The Rawafah and Dissah sites will keep you busy all day Thursday. Our suggestion is therefore that you devote your Friday to Al Bad and Qurayah with an 8.00 a.m. departure from your Tabuk base, to make sure you are on time for your evening flight back to Jeddah.

Your day trip starts via Duba, with a pleasant fishing harbour, and Qaal'at al Muwayleh, an Egyptian-Turkish fort. The Al Bad site – others say Mugheir Shueib, Madian (Ptolemy) or Midyan (the early Islamic writers) – is accepted by the specialists as a major stopover on the frankincense road, 100 km north of Rawafah. With 30 Nabatean tombs surveyed in the southern hills of the Al Bad town, it is also nicknamed 'the small Mada'in-Salah'. The Department of Antiquities has not yet opened the site to the public and you have to climb onto the top of your 4 WD to observe the six tombs, noticeable on the western side of the Duba-Haql road. At this point you are able to photograph with a telephoto lens and overcome the obstacle of the fence bordering the road. You then go back to Tabuk in a northerly direction via Ash Sharaf and Bir ibn Hermas and follow Wadi Zeita upstream. On both sides you see sandstone pinnacles. Some parts of the cliff close to the road are regularly used by rock climbers for their routine practice. In this canyon, which is often compared with Wadi Rum in Jordan, you can select the narrow side wadi of your choice as a picnic and resting place. Even during the hottest summer day, coolness in the shade is guaranteed, thanks to a permanent light breeze.

Fifteen kilometres before Bir ibn Hermas, again fences from the Department of Antiquities appear on the south of the road. There, among hills less than 100 m high, are spread the remnants of a Bronze Age village, two Nabatean buildings, a 400 x 300 m Roman oppidum (walled military camp), several cross-country walls, either dams protecting the village area from flash floods or ramparts giving the name of Qurayah (walled hamlet) to this bowl. Specialists suggest that this is a Nabatean agricultural settlement which was abandoned during the 20 to 50-year-long drought circa 600 AD and has never been occupied again, not even later during the Islamic period, as unlike Tabuk the area has no permanent well. This visit is a tribute to the genius of the Nabatean farmers of the Roman era, who used the best techniques to cultivate crops, thanks to the qanat (underground canal) system. Demoralised by several years without rain and crops, the Nabateans moved north towards Syria and Egypt to find more fertile lands.

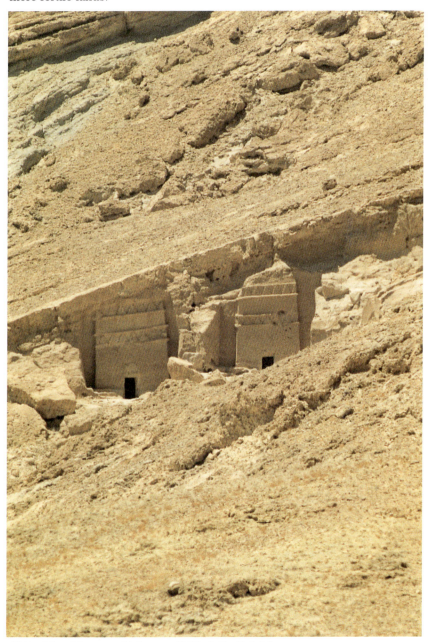

Al Bad is nicknamed 'the small Mada'in-Salah'.

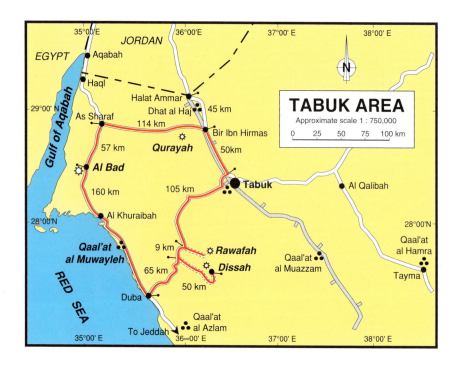

How to get there – refer to the Tabuk area map above.
Rawafah and Dissah
  0 Tabuk Hejaz Railway Station. Go west to Duba.
105 At the signpost 'Rawafah' in Arabic, before a big descent, go south-east on a Bedouin track.
126 **Rawafah** square ruins behind a fence. Mileage to go round the cliffs to find rock carvings is not included. Go back to the Duba road.
147 Back on asphalt. Proceed south for 9 km by the big descent.
156 Petrol station on the left. Ask for confirmation of the Dissah graded dirt track from the station attendant. Take it for 50 km.
206 **Dissah** village, entrance to Wadi Qaraqir.

Al Bad and Qurayah
  0 Tabuk Hejaz Railway Station. Go west to Duba.
179 Duba fishing harbour. Go north to Haql.
229 **Qaal'at al Muwayleh** on left-hand side (west) of the road. Go on north.
339 **Al Bad/Mugheir Shueib**. Before the town, 3 tombs are noticeable 200 m behind the fence on your left (west).
396 As Sharaf, turn right (east) at the road crossing.
496 **Qurayah** fence on right-hand side (south) of the road. The site is 8 km long from north to south and 4 km wide from west to east. Excluding the mileage on site, with 65 km to go back to Tabuk, your circuit is 561 km long.

THE HEJAZ RAILWAY (CFH*)

Starting point: Tabuk exit on Madinah 3rd ring road
Finishing point: Halat Ammar CFH station at the Jordanian border
Distance/Time: 1,440 km/several 3/5-day trips
From Madinah to Mada'in-Salah: 354 km
From Mada'in-Salah to Tabuk: 264 km – From Tabuk to the Jordan
border: 75 km + 750 km to come back to Madinah by road
Category: Four-wheel drive
Highlights: the former rail beds; rail workshops; old locomotives;
mammoth arch rock; Qusaybah dam; many forts; a pilgrims' camp.

Historical background

Sultan Abdel Hamid II (1842-1918), Head of the Ottoman Empire, devoted a
lot of energy to ensure the success of a railway which would transport
hundreds of thousands of pilgrims from Damascus to Madinah and then to
Makkah. The prevailing system in the Empire at the end of the 19th
century had been to concede a busy line to a foreign company, either
British, German or French. After several such concessions, leaving to
foreigners the technical responsibilities and the commercial profits, the
Sultan was convinced that the time had come for the Ottomans to master
such an engineering project.

The financial aspect was most original. The Muslim world and the
Ottoman Government Service, at all levels, were strongly invited to
contribute part of their salary. Other resources were also assigned to the
project, such as the sale of a special issue of stamps and the sale of skins
from the sheep that were sacrificed during the religious festivals. An
ad hoc board was also created to ensure that all funds raised were used on
the railway project, safe from any high-level greediness.

The first engineering task was to determine the rail route in a very
difficult terrain and this was given to the Ottoman Engineer Corps. The
Turkish officer assigned to the project unfortunately gave too much
emphasis to the Haj camel trail and overlooked the specific limits of the
steam engines. He was fired.

Izzet Pasha, Second Secretary to the Sultan and mastermind of the
project, recommended the recruitment of an experienced engineer,
Heinrich Meissner, a German, who proved himself to be the right choice;
his technical capability was supported by an outstanding understanding of
his Turkish colleagues. All services of the Turkish Forces were mobilised to
supply the best workforce; 7,000 men were assigned to the earthwork and
the laying of sleepers and rails. Masons from Damascus who for centuries
were accustomed to this type of work, achieved an extremely high quality
in both appearance and strength of culverts, bridges, forts for 25 men
every 20 km and barracks for 100 men. Lava and limestones were
beautifully trimmed. Their achievements are still visible today along the
rail bed, echoing their skills and craftsmanship in line with the sturdy
caravanserais which they produced earlier on the same Damascus-Makkah

---

** CFH: French abbreviation standing for 'Chemin de Fer du Hedjaz', painted on the Belgian and
German rolling stock by the French-speaking maintenance people in Damascus.*

Rare are the rails still noticeable along the rail bed.

route. When the building speed was considered to be too slow, Paul Gaudin, a French engineer, was assigned to the project of improving the logistics of the building site which was 500 km from the Damascus base. The main issue was to motivate the workforce and thus accelerate the work speed by giving an incentive to officers and men according to their production. In August 1908 a party of foreign journalists was invited to an inauguration trip from Damascus to Madinah, three days and three nights for a distance of 1,302 km across the Hejaz, instead of two months formerly, with a maximum speed of 60 km an hour.

The rolling stock, like the rail track expertise, had different origins. A specialised periodical, 'the Continental Railway Journal from the United Kingdom', succeeded in making an inventory of the locomotives now left along the way:

- in Madinah workshop, 3 locomotives in a double shed:
  - a 2.8.0 with a French-language warning notice (supposed to be a Schweitzrische Locomotive & Machinenfabrick/SLM product).
  - another 2.8.0. without marking left.
  - a 2.6.0.
- at Buwayr station, 100 km north of Madinah, a freight train standing in the station with the locomotive No. 101, a Hartmann 2.8.0. built in 1910 and in 1921 appearing on a list as 'a property of the Syrian Railway Company'.
- at Hadiyah station, 78 km north of Buwayr, the locomotive now lying in the sand on a siding is a Krauss built 0-6-0 T No. 17.
- in between Wayban and Muduraj, 72 km south of Zumrud, the

The Buwayr CFH station and its train are easy to visit.

57

derailed locomotive is well identified as the SLM No. 151, a 2.8.0. overrun by its tender, which now lies a short distance in front.
- in the Mada'in-Salah workshop, a Jung 2.6.0. No. 6 built in 1906.
- at Halat Ammar, 2 km south of the Jordan border and 110 km north of Tabuk, lies a Hartmann 2.8.0. No. 110 without tender.

In many places railway carriages, from Morlanwelz in Belgium, are visible in various conditions, but the only one showing its wooden shell is the one standing at the Al Ula station.

From 1908 to 1924, many ambushes produced casualties such as this one, found close to al Muduraj.

What happened between the Turkish-European pride of the 1908 inauguration and the closure of the traffic in 1924? In 1914 the Allied Forces were engaged in a fratricide war with imperial Germany. The Young Turks in power from 1909 onwards favoured siding with their German partners. The British, the French and the Arabs of Hejaz favoured keeping the Turks and Germans away from the Suez Canal. Sherif Hussein, the Hashemite king, and his sons Ali, Abdallah and Faisal, General Allenby, T.E. Lawrence, Col. Bremond, Capt. Pisani – the French artillery officer – were all figureheads of the Hejaz operations.

T.E. Lawrence, the archaeologist devoted to Syrian antiquities turned desert warlord, conceived guerrilla tactics approved by Her Majesty's Arab Bureau in Cairo at the Spring of 1917. According to 'The Seven Pillars of Wisdom', Turkish trains were ambushed on March 29, at Abu Naam and on April 5, 1917 at km 1,121 north of Muduraj. Then T.E. Lawrence focused on

Damascus and left the containment of the Turks in their Madinah and Al Ula strongholds to his Arab, British and French partners.

Two attempts were made by the Kingdom in the sixties and the seventies to rebuild the track using a Japanese company, starting from Madinah and later a British and Spanish company starting from Jordan. What is left from these attempts are derelict yellow trucks from Bir Nasif to Abu Taqah and different building techniques, concrete pipes instead of stone culverts in the south and wooden railway sleepers from Australia in the north.

The six-day war of 1967 and accumulation of financial and construction problems only foiled the revival of the line, considering also that airlines and road transportation now adequately cope with the three million pilgrims arriving in Makkah during the Haj period.

A tentative programme

If the title of this chapter is restricted to the Hejaz Railway for ease of comments, the common practice is to add to the pleasure of the trip by visiting archaeological and natural sites on the way, for instance:

- a sample of railway at Buwayr (see page 63).
- good physical exercise by climbing the Jebel Antar (see pages 63-64).
- a sample of the camel period with the Shajwa caravanserai (see page 78).

Hereunder we suggest a five-day programme which covers the Madinah - Mada'in-Salah section (see page 63) of the CFH. The schedule could be:

Day 1
- Start from Jeddah North meeting point at 9.00 a.m.
- Follow the freeway to Madinah.
- Go through the two Madinah (south and north) police checkpoints before lunch.
- Picnic in the shade of Hafirah CFH station, only 4 km north-west of the northern Madinah checkpoint.
- Take a break at the Qusaybah dam 23 km north of the square minaret of Salsalah. The dam is only 2 km east of the road by a roughly asphalted track (see page 85).
- Go to Al Ula by the well-indicated road.
- Arrive before the evening at the 'Mammoth', a huge stone arch halfway between Al Ula and Mada'in-Salah (see Mada'in-Salah and Al Ula map, page 47). Lovely camping, but be ready for rain at night. It happens without warning, some sandy flats can become lakes.

Day 2
- Full day devoted to the Mada'in-Salah site (see page 38). The major railway station is a perfect introduction to the full railway.
- Second camping at the 'Mammoth'.

Day 3
- First slice of the railway track from Wadi Hashish appearing east of the road among palm trees, to Zumrud CFH station.

The 'Mammoth', a pleasant camping site east of Wadi Hashish CFH station.

- Day devoted to Al Ula (see page 48) and the quick visit of the three CFH stations before Zumrud.
- Camping behind the railway fort and the ballast heaps of Zumrud.

Day 4

- Go south to Bir el Jedid CFH fort (see page 65) and this offers you a leap into the past at Qaal'at as Sawrah, 2.7 km south-east of the CFH fort (see page 74).
- Come back on to the rail bed and visit all the stations down to Abu Naam and its well.
- Hadiyah station is worth a long stop and a picnic.
- Camp somewhere in the wide valley away from the traffic bordering the rail bed at the level of Abu Naam.

Day 5

- Enjoy the railway down to Qaal'at Muheit, the last station before

Madinah (see Madinah West map, page 46). The Muheit site is convenient for picnics. When you go down to the Madinah ring road either on the rail bed or by reverting to the Tabuk-Madinah road through a 3-km-long dirt track towards the east, you feel like a pilgrim about to enter the Holy City.

- You have the afternoon to complete the last 400 km bringing you back to Jeddah and your "Home, Sweet Home"!

Wadi Hashish CFH fort.

Warning

No other cross-country field trip is easier to perform than this one without getting lost, thanks to the rail bed guideline, but...

- do not stay on the rail bed when there are no fresh car tracks on it. This means that you are approaching a dangerous gap in the rail bed. You may crash your vehicle in an unexpected gap of the rail bed. It has already happened. We do not wish this to happen to you.
- Do not follow the lovely Bedouin tracks which look faster without keeping an eye on the rail bed. Some Bedouin tracks start parallel to the rail bed, then suddenly go to a village far away from the rail bed.
- Avoid camping too close to the forts. The desert police may take you for a 'treasure hunter' looking for the concealed savings of the poor chaps of the railway line left to themselves when the Turkish Army collapsed in the Damascus area in October 1918.

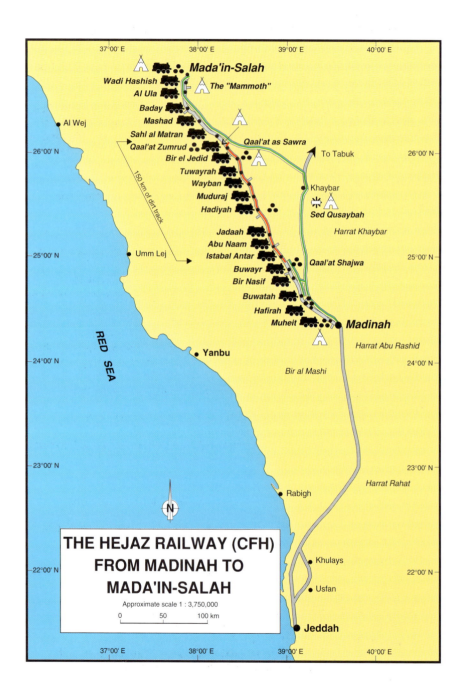

**THE HEJAZ RAILWAY (CFH)
FROM MADINAH TO
MADA'IN-SALAH**

Approximate scale 1 : 3,750,000

0   50   100 km

37°00' E   38°00' E   39°00' E   40°00' E

Mada'in-Salah

Wadi Hashish
Al Ula   The "Mammoth"
Baday
Mashad
Sahl al Matran
Qaal'at Zumrud   Qaal'at as Sawra
Bir el Jedid   To Tabuk
Tuwayrah
Wayban   Khaybar
Muduraj
Hadiyah   Sed Qusaybah

Harrat Khaybar

Jadaah
Abu Naam
Istabal Antar   Qaal'at Shajwa
Buwayr
Bir Nasif
Buwatah
Hafirah
Muheit   Madinah

Harrat Abu Rashid

Al Wej

Umm Lej

150 km of dirt track

26°00' N   26°00' N
25°00' N   25°00' N

RED SEA

Yanbu

Bir al Mashi
24°00' N   24°00' N

23°00' N   23°00' N

Harrat Rahat

Rabigh

N

Khulays
22°00' N   22°00' N
Usfan

Jeddah

62

How to get there

SECTION 1/3: FROM MADINAH TO MADA'IN-SALAH (MAY 1995)

Madinah, CFH station No. 1

Main station in the city centre. The front wall was still in existence in 1995. Non-Muslims are not allowed. Workshop, double shed (Tabuk type), 4 tracks, 3 locomotives in 1986.

Coming from Jeddah by the Madinah 3rd ring road, the foreign traveller has no way of identifying the former rail bed when it crosses the ring road. East of the ring road, it is now a radial street going to the city centre. West of the ring road, it is a government built-up area covering 2 km of former rail bed. Therefore the access to CFH station No. 2 is by its northern face (for 2 WD also), provided the unpaved section has not been damaged by fresh heavy rain.

0 Enter the area by the 'Tabuk' exit on the Madinah 3rd ring road (see Madinah West map, page 46), coming either from Jeddah or from Madinah Sheraton Hotel.
Go north-west for 9 km.

9 Turn left into the unsigned private paved road going to the compound of a building contractor (+ 600 m).
Go west by a dirt track passing through a garbage dumping area.
When you meet the rail bed 3 km west of the Tabuk road, go south for 2 km on the rail bed.

14 **Qaal'at Muheit or Makhit, CFH station No. 2**
Small fort (25 men) + barracks (100 men) + auxiliary forts on the surrounding hills. Recommended **camping area** 1 km south-west of the railway fort. Go back to take the Madinah-Tabuk road, heading north.

31 Police checkpoint, north of Madinah.
Turn left into a secondary road with the sign 'Hafirah' (+ 400 m).

35 **Hafirah, CFH station No. 3**
(same name as a **caravanserai** 4 km north-east, see page 73).
Small fort (25 men) + barracks (100 men).
Go on along the rail bed but be aware there is a 15-km unpaved section before Buwatah.

55 **Buwatah, CFH station No. 4**
Small fort (25 men) + barracks (100 men).
You can now follow a parallel paved road for 50 km up to Shajwa.

75 **Bir Nasif, CFH station No. 5**
Small fort (25 men) + damaged barracks (100 men) with enlarged gate for truck entrance.

95 **Buwayr, CFH station No. 6**
Barracks (100 men) + small fort (25 men) + water tower + loading dock + housing + ballast heaps + entire train on its rails (locomotive + 10 carriages + tender in the rear).

105 End of tarmac. **Qaal'at Shajwa** 7 km east (see page 73 and map on page 78). Top up your petrol tank at Shajwa.

115 **Istabal Antar, CFH station No. 7**
Small fort (25 men) + barracks (100 men). Jebel Antar appears in the west (see map overleaf: easy climbing from the campsite to the south molar).

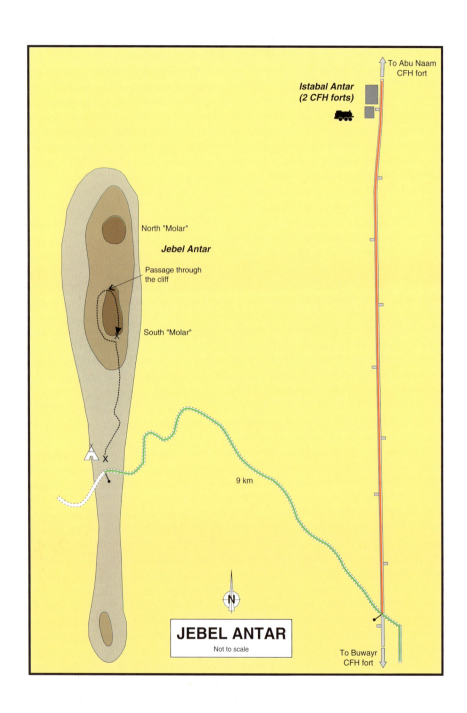

To Abu Naam
CFH fort

**Istabal Antar
(2 CFH forts)**

North "Molar"

Jebel Antar

Passage through
the cliff

South "Molar"

9 km

X

N

JEBEL ANTAR
Not to scale

To Buwayr
CFH fort

64

135 Abu Naam, CFH station No. 8
Small fort (25 men) + water tower + barracks (100 men). Recent restoration carefully done. Bir (well) very much in use. Read chapter 34 of 'The Seven Pillars of Wisdom' by T.E. Lawrence.

156 Jadaah, CFH station No. 9
Small fort (25 men) + 2 Belgian-made carriages + destroyed or unfinished barracks (100 men). Wide pass.

176 Hadiyah, CFH station No. 10
Marshalling station + setting for battalion on the ridges + water tower + 2 small forts (15 and 25 men) + train on its side + upright train set with 5 Belgian-made carriages with interesting markings. **Two old qaal'ats** are 8 km east (see page 73 and map on page 79).

193 Muduraj, CFH station No. 11
Small fort (25 men) + water tower + small fort (15 men). Mentioned in 'The Seven Pillars of Wisdom' by T.E. Lawrence.
Locomotive + tender + damaged Belgian made carriage (+ 7 km).

205 Wayban, CFH station No. 12
Small fort (15 men) of lava stone + a 10-m-long cistern for flat bed carriages.

217 Tuwayrah, CFH station No. 13
Small fort (25 men) + water tower + small fort (15 men) + 1 Belgian-made carriage on its side.

234 Bir el Jedid, CFH station No. 14
Small fort (25 men). The old **Qaal'at as Sawrah** is 2.5 km towards the south-east, visible intermittently behind a double-head hillock (see page 74 and map on page 81).

253 Dry well, 16-m-deep + cistern from station water tower. This well is isolated on the side of the rail bed without any other building.

258 Zumrud, CFH station No. 15
Small fort (25 men) + stock of ballast, under a rectangular microwave reflector, visible 500 m south of the road. Mentioned in 'The Hejaz in the World War' by the General Bremond, Head of the French mission in the Middle East from 1916 to April 1918. The old **Qaal'at Zumrud** is 4.5 km towards the west (see page 74 and map on page 82).

269 A single tender, 200 m south of the road.

272 Sahl al Matran, CFH station No. 16
Small fort (25 men), visible 400 m south of the road.

299 Mashad, CFH station No. 17
Small fort (25 men), 100 m south of the road, opposite a petrol station.

312 Baday, CFH station No. 18
Station + small fort (25 men) + water tower + windmill. Visible 500 m south of the road.

The Belgian railway carriage at Al Ula.

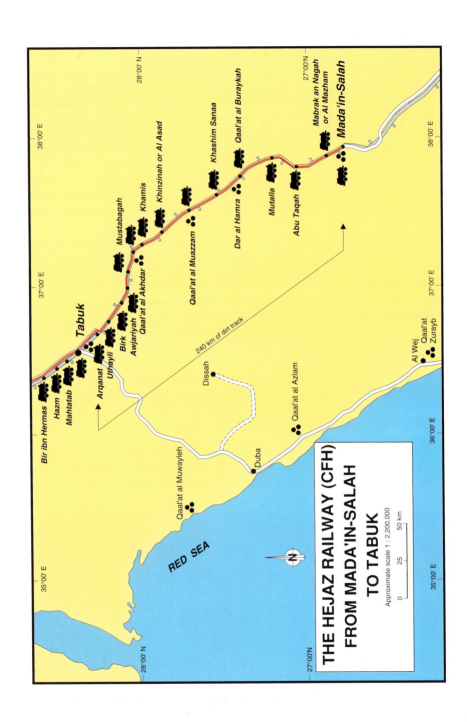

THE HEJAZ RAILWAY (CFH)
FROM MADA'IN-SALAH
TO TABUK

Approximate scale 1 : 2,200,000

0   25   50 km

RED SEA

Bir ibn Hermas
Hazm
Mahtatab
Arqanat
Uthayli
Birk
Awjariyah
Qaal'at al Akhdar
Mustabagah
Khamis
Khinzinah or Al Asad
Qaal'at al Muazzam
Dar al Hamra
Khashim Sanaa
Qaal'at al Buraykah
Mutalla
Abu Taqah
Mabrak an Nagah
or Al Mazham
Mada'in-Salah

Tabuk

240 km of dirt track

Dissah

Qaal'at al Muwayleh

Qaal'at al Azlam

Duba

Al Wej
Qaal'at
Zurayb

35°00' E
36°00' E
37°00' E
38°00' E

28°00' N
27°00' N

66

333 **Al Ula,**
CFH station No. 19
Main station + small
fort (25 men) with
tiled roof + windmill +
water tower +
Belgian-made
carriage with boards.

344 **Wadi Hashish,**
CFH station No. 20
Small fort (25 men)
found inside the
village, behind palm
trees.

354 **Mada'in-Salah,**
CFH station No. 21
Main workshop +
small fort (25 men) +

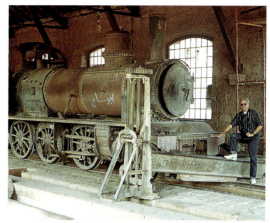

The Jung engine kept in the Mada'in-Salah CFH workshop.

underground stores for explosives + housing + Rheinland locomotive +
tender + 4 Belgian-made carriages + water tower. These buildings are
next to the **Islamic pilgrimage fort** (qaal'at) of the caravan era (see
page 75).

SECTION 2/3: FROM MADA'IN-SALAH TO TABUK (MAY 1993)
  0 **Mada'in-Salah (780 m altitude), CFH station No. 21**
Main workshop + small fort (25 men) + underground stores for explosives
+ housing + Rheinland locomotive + tender + 4 Belgian-made carriages +
water tower. These buildings are next to the Islamic pilgrimage fort (see
page 75) of the caravan era.

14 **Mabrak an Nagah or Al Mazham, CFH station No. 22**
Small fort (25 men) featuring a porch with 3 arched openings at the foot
of the cliff. West wall collapsed following subsequent floods.

18 Hairpin of the railway in leaving the valley for the plateau eastward.
The automobile track avoids the sand dunes covering the railway line by
branching off 500 m ahead into a graded and stone-lined road.

32 **Abu Taqah (970 m altitude), CFH station No. 23**
Small fort (25 men) on the
plateau.

54 **Mutalla (1,141 m altitude),**
CFH station No. 24
Small fort (25 men) +
wreckage of 2 Belgian-made
carriages.

74 **Qaal'at al Buraykah or**
Dar al Hamra, CFH
station No. 25
Small fort (25 men)
featuring porch with 3 arched
openings + 4 Belgian-made
carriages (one utility Turkish

This train was definitely Turkish.

WC). At 2 km eastward sharp and very jagged sierra. **Dar al Hamra** caravanserai is behind a ridge 2.5 km south-west of the CFH fort.

86 Huge ballast stock.

101 **Khashim Sanaa, CFH station No. 26**
Small fort (25 men) featuring porch with 3 arched openings and ballast stock. Fort from the caravan era set on top of an isolated hill 1 km to the east with an area reserved for 30 round pilgrims' tents.

115 Hamlet with police station, petrol station.

126 **Qaal'at al Muazzam (967 m altitude), CFH station No. 27**
Small fort (15 men), ground level construction featuring porch with 3 arched openings + housing + water tower + Belgian-made carriage reduced to 2 bogies + triangular-shaped siding track.

127 Splendid **caravanserai** with 4 corner towers + open-air cistern (protected by Government-provided enclosure) + long water-collecting dam at the edge of an immense flat depression + more recent windmill. Fortifications on ridges all around. Modern open-air cistern west of the station where in May lorries come to draw water for the flocks.

148 Fort of the caravan era on east ridge.

151 **Khinzinah or Al Asad (1000 m altitude), CFH station No. 28**
Small fort (15 men) with fortifications for a full infantry battalion on the ridges.

154 Ballast stock.

167 Pilgrims' or labourers' camp: approximately 20 round huts with stone foundations between cliff and railway embankment.

174 **Khamis, CFH station No. 29**
Small fort (25 men) featuring porch with 3 arched openings secured by fortifications on the ridges. Double railway track for crossing.

The Turkish soldiers received extra pay based on the amount of ballast extracted, as measured by the still-visible square heaps.

68

This tunnel is still very much in use.

180 **Fort** of the caravan era on the west ridge with areas set for tents and approach ramp to the north.

192 **Qaal'at al Akhdar, CFH station No. 30**
Small inhabited fort (25 men) + 300 m of overturned rails below the embankment + sub-frame of Belgian-made carriage. Collapsed caravanserai and open-air cistern, both protected by Government-provided enclosure.
Police station north of a long bridge.

198 **Mustabagah, CFH station No. 31**
Small fort (15 men), building stripped of facing stones on the slope towards the 130-m-long tunnel.

200 **Awjariyah, CFH station No. 32**
Small fort (25 men) featuring porch with 3 arched openings, secured by fortifications on the ridges. Double track for crossing.

212 **Birk, CFH station No. 33**
Small fort (15 men) featuring porch with 3 arched openings. Ground level construction.

224 **Uthayli, CFH station No. 34**
Small fort (15 men) featuring porch with 3 arched openings. Ground level construction + ballast stock. Track maintained to provide access to a microwave tower on the ridge south-west of the station.

236 **Arqanat, CFH station No. 35**
Small fort (25 men) featuring porch with 3 arched openings.
242 Asphalted road.
248 New dual lane road
261 Crossroads at the entrance to Tabuk with 2 monumental tanks.
264 **Tabuk (777 m altitude), CFH station No. 36**
Renovated station + workshop in town.

Awjariyah, a CFH soldier fort.

Caravanserai 2 km westward which was repaired in 1994.

SECTION 3/3: FROM TABUK TO THE JORDAN BORDER (AUGUST 1994)

0 **Tabuk, CFH station No. 36**
Go north and follow the sign 'Jordanian border'. Stay on the asphalt road.
15 **Mahtatab, CFH station No. 37**
4 arches, ground floor only.
Great modern farms, mainly on east side of the road.
30 **Hazm, CFH station No. 38**
4 arches, ground floor only.
Eastwards appears a mountain nicknamed 'The Prophet's Pulpit'.
50 **Bir ibn Hermas, CFH station No. 39**
4 arches, ground floor only + a one-tank water tower.
Leave the road going north-east on the plateau and stick to the rail bed.
65 **Dhat al Haj, CFH station No. 40**
4 arches, ground floor only, recently occupied + water tower + windmill.
This former border post located in a small oasis is now uninhabited.
Qaal'at Dhat al Haj is 500 m south-east of the CFH station (see page 77). From here the rail track has been rebuilt in the 1960s with wooden sleepers from Australia.
75 **Halat Ammar, CFH station No. 41**
4 arches, ground floor only + a locomotive lying on its side 300 m south of the station + crude fort on the hill lying east.
The rail track goes north towards Al Mudawara in Jordan.
The Saudi border post is 1 km north. We recommend that you do not follow the rail bed up to the border. Take the east road and come back to Tabuk by the asphalt road.

SYRIAN HAJ CARAVANSERAIS

> **Starting point:** Jeddah north, police checkpoint on Madinah freeway
> **Finishing point:** Dhat al Haj
> **Distance/Time:** 2,580 km (2 WD), 2,150 km (4 WD)/a 4-day trip
> **Category:** Two and four-wheel drive
> **Highlights:** many qaal'at (castle) ruins, formerly resthouses for Haj
> pilgrims and caravans; the Hejaz Railway and old rail beds; Nabatean site.

When the normal means of transportation was riding a donkey, a horse, a dromedary or even just walking, depending on your wealth, the Faith was already driving thousands of pilgrims to travel during some two months from Damascus to Makkah and back. This is the Haj route of the Syrians, also named Darb al Tabukiyah via Tabuk, Al Hijr (Mada'in-Salah) and Madinah.

Historical background
Along the route, the Department of Antiquities and Museums from the Ministry of Education of the Kingdom has surveyed several qaal'ats (castles*) or caravanserais of obvious Syrian influence deserving a protective fence (they are here mentioned with the sign #). According to the dictionary, caravanserai is a word of Persian origin meaning an inn where caravans rest at night, that is commonly a large bare building surrounding a courtyard, usually in a small oasis. Unfortunately the scientific dating of these structures is not yet known. Are they of the Omayed period (661-750 AD)? Are they of the Ottoman period which started in the Arabian peninsula in the 16th century?

The Turkish rule in the peninsula ended in January 1919 with the surrender of the Madinah garrison to the armies of Sherif Hussein, the Hashemite King of Hejaz from 1916 to 1920. Certainly, the three centuries before 1919 saw the Wali of Damascus in charge of the supply and maintenance of the 'motels' of the Syrian route. Each qaal'at is a special case and has been built and refurbished sometime in between 700 and 1980 (in the case of Qaal'at al Hijr/Mada'in-Salah).

How to visit the caravanserais
A field trip starting from Madinah and finishing at the border with Jordan will give you an insight into the hardship and marvels of the Haj in the old days, before the age of cars, trains and aircraft. To discover the ancient achievements of the 'motel' type accommodation of that time, a 4 WD vehicle is a must in order to be able to follow the Hejaz railway track (CFH) as a guide. Some Haj qaal'ats can be visited by travellers with a 2 WD vehicle by using another and longer way than the CFH rail bed. In that case they are mentioned with the sign '2 WD' and their visit constitutes an alternative field trip mentioned after the 4 WD route. This description is limited to Haj caravanserais, but the route followed has many other attractive spots deserving attention in a trip not dedicated to just qaal'ats (see the Hejaz Railway route, page 55).

The list of the qaal'ats surveyed by the Department of Antiquities has been published in ATLAL, the journal of Saudi Arabian archaeology, volume 7, dated 1403 AH – 1983 AD.

A stairway leading to the watchman gallery at Qaal'at al Muazzam.

Qaal'at Hafirah (2 WD)

This caravanserai is visible 6 km north of the northern Madinah police checkpoint, from the road leading to Khaybar. It is accessed via a 700-m-long graded dirt track which starts on the western side of the Madinah-Khaybar road, after a white mosque. The main structure of black lava stone is 21 x 21 m and some 6 m high. The entrance opens onto a roofless courtyard of 12 x 4 m with several rooms on the left-hand side and right-hand side and a stairway leading to the roof around which you find a 2-m-high parapet with battlements. All around this central building there is a 3-m-high outer wall leaving a 3-m-wide passageway on the 4 sides. This wall has only one door, 1.7-m-wide, and several arrow slits for observation and defence. The architecture is so simple that many times you may pass by close to this qaal'at without guessing the purpose of this square low building at the edge of a palm grove in the wide bed of Wadi Hamd. The luxury of this caravanserai is that it has its own well inside a corner of the outer defensive wall. This design is representative of several other caravanserais appearing farther in the north, that are considered as the oldest and the poorest of the early supply line of the so-called Syrian pilgrims' route.

Qaal'at Abiar al Nasif (2 WD)

This caravanserai is of the Hafirah type, but much more damaged. To find it among the farms north of Mulayleh, you may need the help of a local shepherd. These ruins are on the south bank of Wadi Rashad, well indicated by a signpost on the east side of the Mulayleh-Buwayr road.

Qaal'at Shajwa (2 WD)

Here you discover a noble 25 x 25 m castle on the low bank of a wide wadi at the northern edge of Shajwa village. It may be compared to Qaal'at Zumrud for the many points they have in common: the beauty of the pointed vaults supporting the watchman gallery in the inner courtyard, the 10-m-high walls plastered with a gypsum layer and towers at some corners, here four but three of them crumbled. Painted or not, the plaster has a light brown colour reflecting the sun's heat. This is also a common practice in the Algerian Sahara to reduce the temperature inside the caravanserai by several degrees centigrade. The entrance has a round arch bearing the inscription 'Allah Othman Mansur' in Arabic. Only 800 m east from the asphalt road, this qaal'at is easy to reach by visitors using an ordinary car and ready to walk a short distance under the palm trees.

The Hadiyah 'Pentagon'.

73

Qaal'at Hadiyah (#)

When you leave Hadiyah CFH railway station due east and follow the meanders of Wadi Khaybar along 8 km, 2 caravanserais suddenly appear. On the northern bank, planted on a 10-m-high rock, is the first caravanserai, an irregular pentagon. In the sandy river bed, 400 m south of the first one, are the ruins of a Hafirah-type caravanserai, so similar that there is nothing to be added. Even with four out of five towers lying on the ground, the pentagon is very impressive, a pilgrim's dream in a green environment contrasting with the austere black skyline at the edge of a harrat in the south-east. Unfortunately you will have to wait for the end of the Department of Antiquities' scientific survey to know the age of the two structures. The pleasure of the visit is reserved to travellers equipped with a 4 WD vehicle, Hadiyah being 70 km north of the Shajwa asphalt road end.

Qaal'at as Sawrah (2 WD)

Standing at the entrance to a mountainous amphitheatre on a soft red carpet of silt, this qaal'at has the size and

Qaal'at as Sawrah: a caravanserai with the shape of a WW II blockhaus.

the architectural features of the Mada'in-Salah Islamic fort: a cubic block of 21 x 21 m, four corbels supported by machicolation, one overlooking a huge 15-m-deep well and another one over the gate, made for pouring unpleasant stuff on the heads of unfriendly visitors knocking too hard at the door. The 8-m-wide outside well is beautifully lined with limestone and is duplicated by an inner well covered by a shed. Visible from the rail bed running 1 km south-west of it, this qaal'at can also be reached from the north by a 10-km-long graded dirt track. This other pilgrim's dream is now a recommended tourist delight.

The gate of Qaal'at Zumrud.

Qaal'at Zumrud (# 2 WD)

South of the Khaybar-Al Ula road, this castle can be reached either from the north by a 3-km-long graded dirt track acceptable for ordinary cars or from the east by a 4.5-km-long Bedouin track starting from the CFH railway fort of Zumrud. Square, plastered with gypsum, with arches around the inner courtyard, towers attached at some of the corners and a birqat (rain water reservoir), are the caravanserai's main features. This qaal'at is a reference showing differences from the Mada'in-Salah type without any towers. Too close to a wadi in a narrow valley, the eastern wall has been heavily damaged by several flash floods.

Mada'in-Salah Islamic Fort (# 2 WD)

Side by side with a CFH railway workshop, Qaal'at Mada'in-Salah (Qaal'at al Hijr) is so nicely rebuilt that it was first believed to be a Disneyland marvel copied from somewhere else for the sake of tourists attracted by the famous Nabatean tombs. This was proved wrong by the 1911 photograph by a train traveller: the qaal'at appears then as the sturdy cube

it is now, with the same pointed vaults and corbels. Earlier in 1874, a British traveller, Charles Doughty, was accommodated in that fort during two months while studying the Nabatean tombs nearby. His detailed description with drawings attached matches perfectly the present copy of the now well-known original caravanserai destroyed to the ground in the 1930s.

Qaal'at al Hijr rebuilt.

Qaal'at al Muazzam (#)

At the edge of a dried mud lake, Qaal'at al Muazzam is the pearl of the caravanserais on the Damascus-Makkah Haj route. Its 60 x 60 m birqat (rain water reservoir) has been improved during the CFH railway period (1900-1908) by the addition of a pumping station operated by a windmill. This reservoir is fed by a 600-m-long dam collecting the rain water falling

fairly regularly on the huge flat area on the south-west of the qaal'at. This caravanserai is the best in terms of quality of the limestone trimming and the number of architectural details:

- an entrance with a pointed vault, a corbel and a plate bearing inscriptions in Arabic letters.
- a well in the middle of the inner courtyard.
- arches to support the stairway and the watchman gallery.

Qaal'at al Muazzam and its birqat.

- a prayer room with a mirhab on the first floor.
- a tower at each of the 4 corners.
- arrow slits on every wall.

On the way from Tayma to Tabuk in February 1884, Charles Huber, the French traveller, spent one night here and mentioned 1031 AH as the year of the building that was written on the stone, which means 1622 AD. He felt sad that three out of the four cupolas over the towers were broken down.

Unfortunately you need a 4 WD vehicle to travel the 130 km of rough dirt track to reach this marvel from either Mada'in-Salah or Tabuk.

Qaal'at Tabuk, dated by a plate over the gate.

Qaal'at Tabuk (2 WD)

This caravanserai is of the Mada'in-Salah type with a plus: glazed tiles over the entrance show a date. In 1062 AH, a Sultan gave the order to rebuild a fort stronger and more beautiful than the former one. In 1988 the western wall crumbled when the birqat cleaning was under way. Now the damage has been repaired and the qaal'at is on the list of the archaeological sites open to the public. The water supply is puzzling because this caravanserai is not along a wadi but on a slight elevation which in the old days gave a long view over the Tabuk plain. Now the fort is in town at the junction between the commercial area and a residential area.

Written in Arabic above the Qaal'at Tabuk gate:

"His Excellency the Wali, son of Sultan Mohamed Khan, in memory of Al Ibrahim Khan ibn Sultan Ahmed Othman, gives to Mohamed ibn...servant of God, the honour of managing this holy fort's reconstruction (Qaal'at Moubarak). God bless him. Ordered in Damascus in Shams (northern country) in the year 1062 of Hegira"
(1652 AD).

76

Dhat al Haj.

Dhat al Haj (2 WD)

The access is by the road going from Tabuk to the border with Jordan. Some 60 km north of Tabuk a signpost mentioning Jagat al Hal marks the entrance to a 5-km-long graded dirt track going to the qaal'at on the west side of the road. From far away, in the middle of a decaying palm grove, you notice the sturdy cube of the caravanserai close to a standard CFH railway station. Here also the wall on the birqat side is crumbling, but inside you recognise a Mada'in-Salah type qaal'at with arches and a watchman gallery.

From Madinah to the border with Jordan, you cover the Syrian pilgrims' route in three days of cautious driving along the Hejaz railway track. But each qaal'at deserves a weekend camping in its neighbourhood in order to have a better knowledge of its environment and to improve the photographs by taking them at different times of the day with different light conditions. We wish you a temperature as nice as the one we experienced in April, which allowed us to have a night's rest in the open.

How to get there with a 4 WD vehicle
We have indicated the Global Positioning System (GPS) coordinates of some of these landmarks.

0 Petrol station and police checkpoint north of Jeddah on Madinah freeway. Up to km 406, refer to page 44.

406 Police checkpoint north of Madinah on Tabuk road.

412 At the T-crossing after mosque and white compound turn left (west) into graded dirt track, and go on for 700 m.
Qaal'at Hafirah (GPS: 24.36.28 N /39.20.19 W) is 50 m south of the dirt track, 700 m from asphalt road. Come back on the Tabuk road and go north (the mileage on the dirt track is not included).

438 At the T-crossing to Mulayleh turn left (west) to join CFH track on the other bank of Wadi Hamd.

441 At the T-crossing, go north along rail bed.

449 **Qaal'at Abiar al Nasif** (GPS: 24.50.50 N / 39.09.23 W) on south bank of Wadi Rashad: a 2-m-high ruin 1 km east of the road and 3.5 km south-east of CFH station of Bir Nasif.

472 **Buwayr CFH station** on left-hand side.

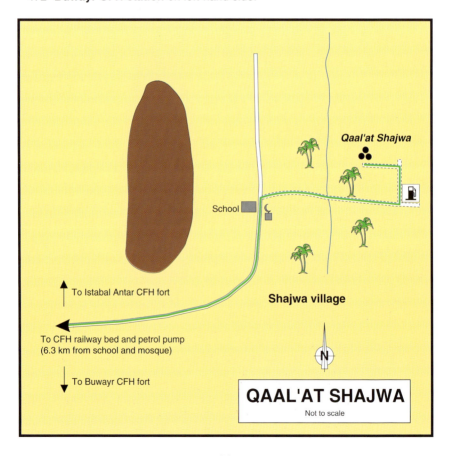

School

Qaal'at Shajwa

To Istabal Antar CFH fort

Shajwa village

To CFH railway bed and petrol pump
(6.3 km from school and mosque)

N

To Buwayr CFH fort

QAAL'AT SHAJWA
Not to scale

78

482 At the T-crossing, go east to Shajwa for 6.3 km on asphalt road.
495 **Qaal'at Shajwa** (GPS: 25.04.00 N / 38.59.71 W)
High cream-coloured wall emerging over the palm tree heads, after
800 m east along a graded dirt track. Go up to a wadi bed and on for
500 m more to reach the qaal'at by its eastern face. Go back to the rail
bed and drive north via Istabal Antar/CFH (+10 km), Abu Naam/CFH
(+15 km), Jadaah/CFH (+13 km), Hadiyah/CFH (+24 km).
1 km before this last station go east to cross a ridge behind which you
will find a police station on the bank of Wadi Khaybar. Follow that wadi
east for another 6 km.

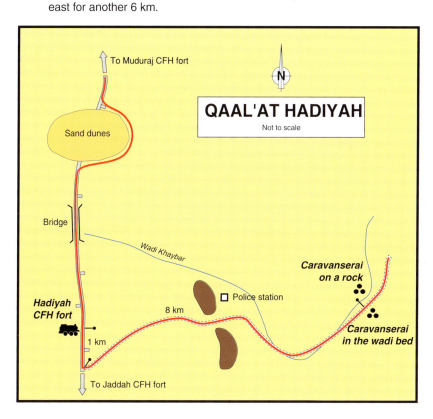

568 **Qaal'at Hadiyah** (GPS: 25.31.64 N / 38.47.95 W)
Go back west to Hadiyah/CFH (+ 8 km). Go north to Muduraj/CFH
(+17 km), Wayban/CFH (+14 km), Tuwayrah/CFH (+14 km), culvert
No. 1301/CFH (+15 km).
100 m before culvert, go north-east for 1.5 km. A square caravanserai
will appear in a breach in the ridge, behind a two-head hillock.
638 **Qaal'at as Sawrah** (GPS: 26.01.34 N / 38.34.96 W)
A track acceptable for ordinary cars, leaving north-east, goes direct to the
Al Ula road some 10 km north (see map on page 81).
Go back north-west to Bir el Jedid/CFH (+2.5 km) and on.

665 Zumrud CFH station

By a Bedouin track starting west behind the CFH fort, go for 3 km and turn north on a better graded track entering a narrow valley with a fenced area at the entrance (ruined structures of unknown nature). Go on 1 km to find the next qaal'at (see map on page 82).

670 Qaal'at Zumrud (GPS: 26.10.25 N / 38.22.92 W)

By the same graded dirt track, go east then, north to the Al Ula asphalted road (+3.5 km) (See map on page 82).

On that road go west to Sahl al Matran/CFH, Mashad/CFH (+27 km), Baday/CFH (+13 km), Al Ula/CFH (+21 km), Wadi Hashish/CFH (+10 km). To proceed to the fenced Nabatean site, you have to produce at the south gate your authorisation from the Department of Antiquities - Ministry of Education/Riyadh.

767 Qaal'at al Hijr / Mada'in-Salah Islamic Fort

You are at the north end of the archaeological site.

To go to the next qaal'at, you have to get out of the Nabatean site by the same south gate and take the ring road by the west.

A heavy traffic graded dirt track starts at a lonely tree north-west of the fence. Follow the west side of the wide wadi going north. After some 5 km a fork will take you east. **Mabrak an Nagah CFH** fort is noticeable on your right-hand side at the base of a cliff. The graded dirt track enters the eastern hills by a hairpin on the right-hand side, 500 m earlier than the rail bed.

Halfway to the top of the plateau, the rail bed reappears on the left from under a big sand dune blown there by the wind. Now stick to the rail bed. Go north via Abu Taqah/CFH, Mutalla/CFH (+22 km), Buraykah/CFH (+20 km), Khashim Sanaa/CFH (+27 km).

Dar al Hamra, a caravanserai visited by Doughty, damaged, but with a birqat still in use, is 2.5 km south-west of Buraykah/CFH. The structure, stripped of its walls, shows the arcades of the stables and demonstrates that this stopover was of the Qaal'at Zumrud level.

Al Muazzam hamlet (+15 km), police station, concrete water tower, petrol pump. Be ready to be asked for your travel letter.

Go north along the rail bed for another 12 km.

893 Qaal'at al Muazzam

After 127 km of dirt track from Mada'in-Salah, the CFH station appears first, then the caravanserai at the base of a hill, easy to climb for photographers.

Go on north via Khinzinah/CFH (+25 km), Khamis/CFH (+23 km), Al Akhdar/CFH (+18 km), Mustabagah/CFH (+6 km), the 130-m-long tunnel, Awjariyah/CFH (+2 km), Birk/CFH (+12 km), Uthayli/CFH (+12 km), Arqanat/CFH (+12 km). The last kilometres of track have been improved, to cater for the traffic created by the maintenance of a microwave tower appearing west on a harrat top. You enter Tabuk on a nice highway running north between 2 military fences. The rail bed is still visible at the end on your right thanks to the stone culverts.

1,031 Qaal'at Tabuk

The caravanserai is 2 km west of the refurbished CFH station, at the upper end of a busy commercial street reserved for pedestrians.

From the Tabuk CFH station, go north following the sign 'Jordanian border'. No need to drive on the rail bed, but stay on the asphalt road and check on your left for the low CFH buildings, Mahtatab (+15 km), Hazm (+15 km), Bir ibn Hermas (+20 km). This station is occupied and fenced.

Keep north on the road to the border. Some 24 km after Bir ibn Hermas crossing, look for a signpost indicating 'Jagat al Hal' on the west. Take that graded dirt track for 5 km.

1,109 **Dhat al Haj**.

An alternative route for 2 WD vehicles

   0 Petrol station and police checkpoint north of Jeddah on Madinah road. Up to km 406, refer to page 44.

406 Police checkpoint north of Madinah on Tabuk road.

412 At the T-crossing after the mosque and white compound turn left (west) into a graded dirt track and go on for 700 m.
Qaal'at Hafirah. Same as 4 WD, page 78.

449 **Qaal'at Abiar al Nasif**. Same as 4 WD, page 78.

490 **Qaal'at Shajwa**. Same as 4 WD to reach the caravanserai, page 79.

542 Go back to the rail bed (+6.3 km) after which you part from the 4 WD road. Go back south to the Tabuk road via Mulayleh. At the Tabuk road, go north towards Khaybar.

659 Al Wadi. Traffic lights and Turkish restaurant. Go on north towards Tabuk.

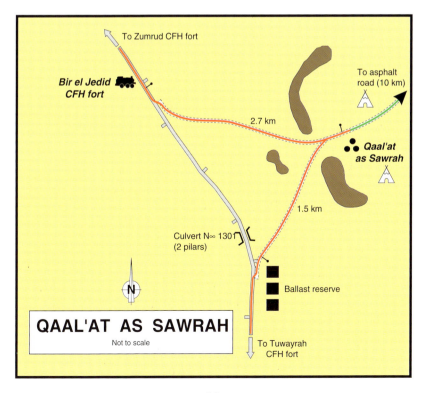

To Zumrud CFH fort

Bir el Jedid CFH fort

To asphalt road (10 km)

2.7 km

Qaal'at as Sawrah

1.5 km

Culvert N∞ 130 (2 pilars)

N

Ballast reserve

QAAL'AT AS SAWRAH

Not to scale

To Tuwayrah CFH fort

81

692 Take 'Al Ula' exit to go west.
744 Ashra, petrol station.
778 Bridge on Wadi Tithan. Crossing with a dirt track (+ 1.3 km). Turn left (west) and go on for 11 km to the caravanserai (see map, page 81).
790 **Qaal'at as Sawrah**
Come back onto the Al Ula road by the same track and go west.
806 Microwave tower, go on for 1.5 km. Crossing with a graded dirt track, go south on that track for 3.4 km up to a **caravanserai**, passing by another fenced archaeological site of unknown nature.
811 **Qaal'at Zumrud**
Same as 4 WD to proceed to the Nabatean site.
913 **Qaal'at al Hijr Mada'in-Salah**
After the qaal'at visit, again your route parts from the 4 WD one. They go north. You go east to join Tayma by the new direct road to Tabuk (and Hail).
1,120 Tayma.
1,398 **Qaal'at Tabuk**. Here again you join the 4 WD route.
1,476 **Dhat al Haj.** By 2 WD you missed only **Qaal'ats Hadiyah**, **Dar al Hamra** and **Al Muazzam.**

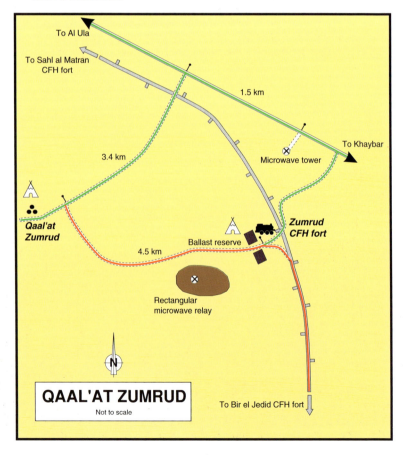

QAAL'AT ZUMRUD
Not to scale

KHAYBAR AND ITS ACROPOLIS

Starting point: Jeddah north, police checkpoint on Madinah freeway
Finishing point: Old Khaybar
Distance/Time: 1,120 km/a 2/3-day trip
Category: Two-wheel drive
Highlights: the old castle of Khaybar; a huge palm grove; a CFH Railway
station and an Omayed dam on the way.

The Khaybar site is left as described by Charles Doughty. He was
'restricted' there for a period of four months by the local Ottoman
representative in November 1877, when his belongings, notebooks,
compass, altimeter and comb (!), were investigated in Madinah. A huge
palm grove fills the cracks opened in the lava field by several wadis. The
black harrat, the abandoned villages, the scorching sun, all give a feeling
of punishment. When you enter the palm grove, life is reappearing, clear
water is running in the channels, a couple of horses are grazing in a
compound, some brand-new metal doors close the access to gardens here
and there. Obviously, the palm grove has some regular visitors, but we did
not meet any during our first three-hour visit. Suddenly, during our
wandering in the maze of alleys a cliff appeared between the palms; we
had discovered Husn Mahrab, the acropolis "200 paces long and 90 paces

Khaybar Acropolis. Doughty saw it the same way 120 years ago.

83

The Qusaybah dam on the Harrat Khaybar.

wide". The old hill is now surrounded by a fence, not open to the public. Rather than giving a detailed description of the site here, we recommend that you sit at the edge of the harrat in front of the acropolis and read the two chapters of Doughty's 'Travels in Arabia Deserta' concerning the old Khaybar, then the old history of this border town of Hejaz will be well understood.

Programme of a visit

In a weekend, your visit to the old Khaybar can be organised as follows:

Day 1
- Departure from Jeddah around 8.00 a.m., picnic at Jebel Mutalata or Qaal'at Muheit, 20 km north west of Madinah and camping at Sed Qusaybah, 140 km north of your Muheit picnic site.

Day 2
- Departure around 9.00 a.m. after early morning photographs of the old 30-m-high dam (history unknown). Visit of old Khaybar starting from the acropolis from 10.00 a.m. to 1.00 p.m. The site is only some 30 km north of Qusaybah dam. Lunch at the Al Wadi bus stop (see mileage chart below).
- Rest stop at Qaal'at Hafirah, 140 km south of Al Wadi and back to Jeddah 450 km south of Hafirah.

How to get there – refer to the Hejaz map, page 4 and also to map overleaf.

0   Petrol station and police checkpoint north of Jeddah on Madinah road. Up to km 406, refer to page 44.
406   Police checkpoint north of Madinah on Tabuk road.
412   At crossing after mosque and white compound turn left (west) onto a graded dirt track. Go west for 700 m. **Qaal'at Hafirah** at 50 m south of the dirt track, 700 m from asphalt road. Come back on the Tabuk road and go north (mileage on dirt track not included).
504   Salsalah main mosque on right-hand side with a square minaret (landmark for Qusaybah dam).
528   Turn right (east) into a roughly asphalted track (23.3 km from Salsalah mosque) Follow the track for 2 km.
530   **Qusaybah dam**, at your feet in a deep gorge.
       To camp on the upstream side of the dam, go back to the Tabuk road and take an old service road towards the south for 800 m along the Madinah road. There, on your left, a 3-km-long winding dirt track brings you east to the **Wadi Thamad bed** and a wide camping area in a palm grove (the mileage to the camping is not included).
534   You are back on the Tabuk road, after a visit to the top of the dam.
540   Thamad main mosque on right with a square minaret (landmark to find the Qusaybah dam when coming from the north).
558   Al Wadi/Ash Shurayf (new Khaybar). Restaurant regularly used by the travellers commuting by bus to Jordan.
560   Turn left (west) at the traffic lights, go left/west for old Khaybar. You are then on the old Tabuk road, now replaced by a 33-km-shorter freeway on the east.
563   Wadi as Sahn: after the new town (Ash Shurayf) and an abandoned

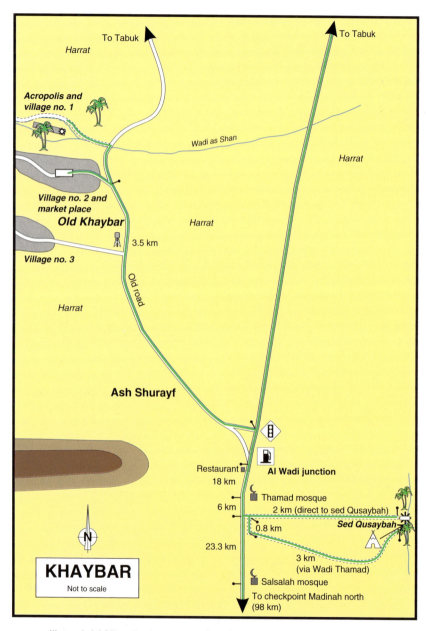

To Tabuk

To Tabuk

Harrat

Harrat

Acropolis and
village no. 1

Wadi as Shan

Village no. 2 and
market place

Harrat

Old Khaybar

3.5 km

Village no. 3

Old road

Harrat

Ash Shurayf

Restaurant
18 km

Al Wadi junction

Thamad mosque

6 km

2 km (direct to sed Qusaybah)

0.8 km

Sed Qusaybah

23.3 km

3 km
(via Wadi Thamad)

Salsalah mosque

N

To checkpoint Madinah north
(98 km)

KHAYBAR

Not to scale

village (**old Khaybar**), you are going down into a huge wadi bed with
plenty of palm trees in poor condition. On the northern side of that wadi,
turn left (west) into a much used dirt track.

564 **Husn Marhab**, the old **Khaybar** acropolis is in front of you.

AL BAHA – DHEE AYN

Starting point: Jeddah, south-east exit on the Makkah freeway
Finishing point: Al Baha Palace Hotel
Distance/Time: 850 km/a 2/3-day trip
Category: Two-wheel drive
Highlights: a variety of watchtowers; primitive beehives inside Kuladah village; an abandoned village; baboons; flowers.

The pleasure of this trip is on the way from Jeddah to Al Baha via Taif along the ridge road. The old watchtowers, which you first discovered in the Taif ash Shafa area, will greet you again all along the way, either as single units in the wild or on top of a fortified village. So this circuit is named 'The thousand and one watchtowers road'. Their logic is always the same – to protect the crops against a greedy neighbour – but they may have some special features:

- Fully crenellated or only the balcony on one side is crenellated.
- Some have a vertical groove on one wall (rainwater drain).
- Some are twins.
- Some are sturdy because they have a wide store.
- Some are as thin as a needle and have a very small storage capability.

In our opinion, the subject deserves a scholar's study. Some specimens are selected here for a stop, but so many others could be the subject of a prize-winning photograph.

Kuladah villages
Seventy kilometres only from Taif's southern checkpoint on Tariq al Junub (the road to the south), two abandoned villages facing each other are overlooking the same wadi where the new village is now settled. Just stop your car on the roadside before the villages and climb the hills up to the watchtowers. On the way, upward or downward, a prayer room, the stables, beehives, balconies with musharabieh are there for you to discover. When you start the visit, the local youth will join you quickly for the pleasure of exchanging a joke with foreigners or helping to find what you are looking for. They never ask for money and often extend an invitation for tea at their home in the new village.

Salba village
A few minutes by car south of Al Baha Palace Hotel and 7 km through a winding road, is an old abandoned village in a dent of the escarpment. The roaming bands of baboons regularly congregate there to play. A pleasant feature of the village is the outside stairways made of stone slabs planted in the walls. From the village a shepherd's path leads down the escarpment to two watchtowers halfway up the slope. It is a pleasant three-hour walk, for people in a good physical condition to visit the two slim towers overlooking the Al Baha-Makwah road. We would advise you to make a morning visit, as in the late afternoon you should avoid being lost in the mist, which comes suddenly from the Tihama plain.

Primitive beehives in the old Kuladah village.

Dhee Ayn, the village on the marble hill

On your way back to Jeddah, go down from Al Baha towards Qilwah via Dhee Ayn, the famous fortified village. Some keen photographers stay at the village for a full day, during which they capture that marvel in various light conditions. With the sun conveniently at the right height, the marble slab separating the top houses from the lower ones at the level of the banana tree really shimmers. To enjoy the visit along the narrow alleys from top to bottom, the spring on the west side of the hill, you have to reserve three hours in your schedule. Be careful to stay away from the shaky houses, as some have already crumbled to the ground.

The shortest road to Jeddah is via Qilwah to join the Tihama road south of Al Lith. This last part of the road is an ongoing pleasure, which deserves a special weekend with camping on the plain on the south bank of Wadi Iliyab.

How to get there – refer also to the Jeddah East map, page 10.

0 'Longines' petrol station at the exit of Jeddah on Makkah freeway. Up to km 182, refer to page 33.

182 Police checkpoint east of Taif. Take direction 'Abha'.

202 Dangerous crossing. Turn right towards 'Bani Saad', to go to al Baha closer to the escarpment than to the direct al Baha road. Stop at any nice old tower and take the photograph you have dreamt about.

250 **Kuladah**, old village No. 1 on right-hand side on the hill.

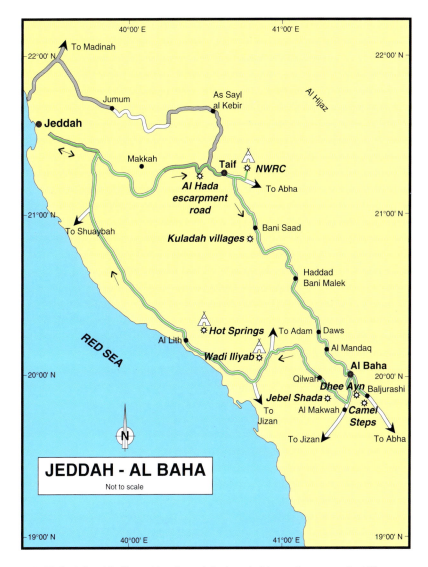

JEDDAH - AL BAHA
Not to scale

252 **Kuladah**, old village No. 2 on right-hand side on the opposite hill.
418 At the junction with the Taif-Al Baha direct road, turn right (south) towards Al Baha.
423 At Al Baha, 1st traffic lights, turn right onto the bridge then left at the 2nd traffic lights. Turn right into the road going to **Raghdan forest**, a public recreation area close to the hotel that you might visit later. At the roundabout, take the first exit to the right going to your resting place.
425 **Al Baha Palace Hotel**. The west rooms are overlooking the escarpment. In the early morning, an army of baboons are begging for a breakfast from the kitchen under your balcony.

How to go back to Jeddah – refer to the Jeddah-Al Baha map, page 89.

- 0 **Al Baha Palace Hotel**. Take direction 'Makwah'.
- 3 Police checkpoint at the entrance to the escarpment descent.
- 10 Car park with a viewpoint on a first fortified village at your feet.
- 28 **Dhee Ayn** village appears suddenly to your left behind a low hill inside a curve on the left. Turn left into a 700-m-long track leading to a car park at the base of the fortified village.
- 47 Before Makwah, turn right (north) towards Al Lith.
- 67 Tunnel entrance. At the exit on left-hand side is a recreation area suitable for picnic side by side with the adeniums obesum.
- 73 Left (west) at the T-crossing, a brand new asphalt road indicated 'Nira' leads you to the ridge within 3 km. There in April/May, you find huge adeniums blossoming (not included in the mileage).
- 75 **Qilwah**, pretty little town. Old fortified villages on both sides of the road.
- 111 Turn left (west) at the T-crossing towards Al Lith.
- 160 Road crossing, you are on the Jizan road. Turn right towards Al Showag and Al Lith.
- 219 Al Lith, traffic lights. The Red Sea is 3.5 km west if you want a rest on the seaside. The **hot springs** (Moyah Ahr) are 47 km to the east, 20 km of graded dirt track beyond Gumayqah.
- 283 Yemeni Meegat. 2 minarets visible from far away. Religious stop for pilgrims coming from the south.
- 344 Shuaybah police checkpoint.
- 383 Junction with the road bypassing Makkah by the south. Turn left.
- 386 Junction with the Makkah-Taif freeway. Turn left.
- 424 'Longines' petrol station. You are back home after an 850-km-long weekend circuit.

Watchtower with a side balcony.

BALJURASHI CAMEL STEPS

Starting point: Al Baha Palace Hotel
Finishing point: Baljurashi camel steps
Distance/Time: 70 km/one day trip
Category: Two-wheel drive
Highlights: a hanging village on the escarpment; camel steps; watchtowers; wild lilies.

From your base in Al Baha, either at the Palace Hotel or camping nearby, a 6-km-long section of the Sarawat escarpment deserves one day of rambling. The Baljurashi camel steps are only 33 km south of the hotel. You will need one hour to cover the distance because the Abha road is very winding and when you go through Baljurashi city it is even more winding. You are in the land of the one thousand and one watchtowers, so on the way you will meet several of these very picturesque buildings, including the twin towers which are the emblem of Al Baha on the city posters.

The camel steps
At the end of the asphalt road you find a car park, very popular for the view you have on the slope of the escarpment. Facing west, a hanging

The Baljurashi camel steps, a scar on the Sarawat flank.

A watchtower on the flat top of a round hillock.

village is on your left-hand side, still inhabited, as may be observed with binoculars. On your right-hand side, the camel steps are winding down, starting from an unfortunate garbage dump. The children usually crave to go down and this is without danger. The paved steps are kept in good condition. Going down 200 m is enough to have a striking view downward and upward. If you feel fit, a walk to the hanging village in the south is worthwhile. Another possibility is to walk along the escarpment. Two watchtowers are worth a picture. South of the pyramidal hill, the tower stands in a pass and is very delicate. The other is laid on the flat top of a round granite hillock and has good control of that section of the escarpment. For that reason, a climb is worthwhile. On the way you may find some lovely natural lilies.

How to get there

0 **Al Baha Palace Hotel**. Return to the traffic lights on the Abha road. There are other routes through town, but they are confusing for a newcomer.
2 Traffic lights on Abha road. Turn south towards Abha.
31 Baljurashi city. After the Nissan workshop, at the traffic lights, turn right into the main street, then follow the maze detailed on the map below.
33 The narrow asphalt road (is it the former camel trail?) reaches the escarpment at a garbage dump from where the **camel steps** trail starts its way down. The car park is 300 m south of the garbage dump.

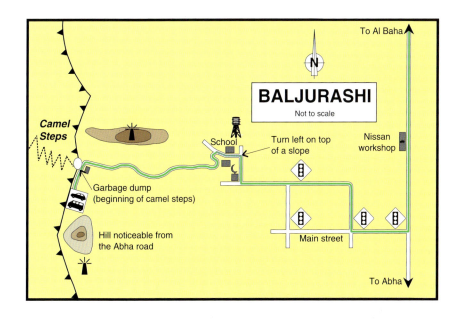

After the 1992 flash flood, a blue car wreck abandoned in a sea of dried mud.

BIBLIOGRAPHY

ATLAL – *The Journal of Saudi Arabia Archaeology* published by the Directorate General of Antiquities and Museums. Ministry of Education, KSA.

BENOIST-MECHIN: *Fayçal, Roi d'Arabie* (1975).
Ibn Séoud, ou la naissance d'un royaume (1955) – Albin Michel.

BREMOND, Edmond, Général: *Le Hedjaz dans la Guerre Mondiale* (1916-1919).

BURCKHARDT, Johann Lewis: *Travels in Arabia, 1814-15* (1829).

COLLENETTE, Sheila: *An illustrated Guide to the Flowers of Saudi Arabia* – Scorpion Publishing Ltd/MEPA.

DIDIER, Charles: *Séjour chez le Grand Chérif de la Mekke, 1857.*

DOUGHTY, Charles M.: *Wanderings in Arabia* – Duckworth.

FARSI ZAKI M.A.: *National Road Atlas and Touring Guide.*

HUBER, Charles: *Journal d'un voyage en Arabie* (1883-1884) – Paris, Imprimerie Nationale.

LAWRENCE, Thomas E.: *The Seven Pillars of Wisdom* – Penguin Book.

MAUGER, Thierry et Danièle: *Heureux bédouins d'Arabie* (1987).
Les hommes-fleurs.

MICHELIN Map No. 954: *Africa, North East, Arabia.*

PESCE, Angelo: *Taif, The Summer Capital of Saudi Arabia* - Immel Publishing.

PHILBY, Harry St. John: *The Land of Midian* – Ernest Benn Limited.

TAMISIER, Maurice: *Voyage en Arabie, séjour dans le Hedjaz, campagne d'Assir, 1840.*

PHOTOGRAPHIC CREDITS

All photographs featured in this book are by the author, except those listed below:

Philippe Baudin -	Page 53	NWRC/Clark Dechant -	Page 35
Michel Bouscary -	Page 17	NWRC/R. Seitre -	Page 29
Edith Guérin -	Page 39	NWRC/Xavier Eichaker -	Pages 25, 28, 30
Dominique Janjou -	Page 56	Jacqueline Truschel -	Page 76
Shirley Kay -	Page 40		
Hélène Legros -	Pages 8, 50, 84, cover image		

Front cover: Dhee-Ayn, the old village with a Tibetan look.
Back cover: Hadiyah railway bridge over Wadi Khaybar.
Title page: Blossoming *adenium* in Jebel Shada al Ala.
Contents spread: Usfan Haj fort on its 'mole hill'.

THE AUTHORS

Roaming around alone in the desert is not Patrick Pierard's cup of tea. Yet his long-lasting desert experiences leave the reader in no doubt as to his feelings towards it. As early as 1959-1961, whilst serving as a young Lieutenant, he patrolled in the eastern and western Algerian Sahara with either a

The authors with their support team. From left: Philip and Sue Bates, Patrick Pierard, Patrick Legros, Dominique Janjou.

motorised platoon of some 30 French draftees or a camel unit of some 20 Reguibat nomads. He tasted the same nomadic life in the Indian desert of Rajasthan with his family of four between 1969-73. Later assigned to Jeddah in 1989, by the Thomson-CSF electronics company, he discovered with delight, what his geologist friends were surveying; wadis, peaks, volcanoes... and all of man's marks left around such as dams, towers, Haj forts and abandoned railway stations.

Born in a family of seven children, he was taught early to share the fruits of life with the others. In 1990 he started a company trekking club, which then became a French Club section, and subsequently a field trip section of the Saudi Arabian Natural History Society of Jeddah. The next step was to write about 'What to see and How to get there' with a wonderful team of reliable friends adding their expertise to his travelling enthusiasm. A professional partnership with Patrick Legros started in 1993 which developed into helping to write this book. Most of the routes have been tested with his 2 WD and his family of four, who validated the driving and camping procedures that the two Patricks have established together.

ACKNOWLEDGEMENTS

Completing this rambling guide was like building a house: We had to find the stones and seek the expertise to assemble them. We are grateful to the strong support team from many professions who contributed to the project. We mention them here alphabetically with their main field of cooperation.

Sue and Philip Bates: Typing and editorial assistance – Edgard Gaspard: Field interpreter in Arabic – Dominique Janjou: Map production, research on CFH railway – André Lorent: Geographical research in Belgium – Major Ali M. Al Maghrabi: Travel administration support and trip adviser – Gérard Montagne: Field trip reconnaissance, drawings – Jean-Pierre Reuter: Early field trip testing – Yolanda and Philip Seddon: NWRC description – Diane and Dan Wood: Saudi Arabian Natural History Society Logistics.

Many others volunteered and contributed their valuable expertise and their names would cover several pages. We thank them all and hope that we may call on them again when one day we attempt to discover more about the country where we live and work. We are especially grateful to Dunlop Tyres whose sponsorship has made possible the publication of this book.